The Ultimate DJ Handbook:

Mastering the Art of DJing

By

Greig Borthwick

DEDICATION

To JonLee my inspiration and guide through the first days on the decks. To the Seattle house music scene 1995! Those were the days. To my sister Megan for putting up with loud crashing beats 24/7. To my loving wife, you weren't even born when I started DJing.
I LOVE YOU!

CONTENTS

10

Chapter 10:

Legal and Ethical Considerations

- Copyright and Licensing
- Respecting Other Artists' Work
- Professionalism and Ethics
- Contracts and Agreements

Chapter 11: Advanced DJing Skills

- Live Remixing and Mashups
- Harmonic Mixing
- DVS (Digital Vinyl Systems)
- DJing with Effects

^

Chapter 1: Getting Started

Welcome to the exciting world of DJing! In this chapter, we'll begin your journey by getting familiar with the essential DJ equipment and the setup process. Whether you're a complete novice or have some prior knowledge, this chapter will lay the foundation for your DJing experience. By the end of this chapter, you'll have a solid grasp of the essential DJ equipment, how to set it up properly, and a fundamental understanding of audio cables. With this knowledge in hand, you'll be well-prepared to move forward in your DJing journey, whether you choose to explore turntables, CDJs, controllers, or a combination of these tools. Get ready to make some noise and start your DJing adventure!

Understanding DJ Equipment

Turntables

The history and significance of turntables in DJ culture:

Turntables, also known as record players, have played a pivotal role in the evolution of DJ culture. Understanding their history and significance is crucial for any aspiring DJ.

- THE BIRTH OF TURNTABLES: The turntable as we know it today has its roots in the late 19th century when the phonograph was invented by Thomas Edison. However, it was not until the mid-20th century that turntables designed for DJ use became prominent.

- THE BIRTH OF DJ CULTURE: The emergence of hip-hop culture in the 1970s in the Bronx, New York, marked a significant turning point for turntables. DJs such as Grandmaster Flash and Kool Herc used turntables to extend and manipulate the breakbeats of songs, giving birth to breakbeat mixing, a foundational DJ technique.

- SCRATCHING AND TURNTABLISM: Turntables also gave rise to turntablism, an art form where DJs use the turntable as an instrument. Scratching, beat juggling, and creative use of the crossfader are essential elements of turntablism.

- VINYL RECORDS AND COLLECTING: Vinyl records have maintained a dedicated following among DJs and audiophiles. The tactile experience of handling vinyl and the unique warmth of analog sound continue to attract DJs to vinyl records.

Different types of turntables, including traditional vinyl and digital vinyl systems (DVS):

Turntables have evolved over time to include various types, catering to different preferences and technological advancements.

- TRADITIONAL VINYL TURNTABLES: These turntables are designed for playing vinyl records. They have a platter, tonearm, cartridge, and stylus for reproducing analog audio from vinyl grooves. Traditional vinyl turntables are favored by vinyl enthusiasts and purists for their authentic sound.

- DIGITAL VINYL SYSTEMS (DVS): DVS technology combines traditional vinyl with digital audio manipulation. DJs use special timecode vinyl records or CDs, which are played on turntables or CDJs and control digital DJ software on a computer. DVS systems offer the flexibility of digital music manipulation while retaining the feel of vinyl.

- HYBRID TURNTABLES: Some modern turntables are designed to work with both traditional vinyl records and DVS systems, allowing DJs to switch between analog and digital formats seamlessly.

Key components of a turntable, such as the tonearm, platter, and cartridge:

To become proficient in DJing, it's essential to familiarize yourself with the key components of a turntable:

- PLATTER: The platter is the rotating part of the turntable where the vinyl record rests. It provides stability and consistent speed for accurate playback.
- TONEARM: The tonearm is the arm-like structure that extends over the platter and holds the cartridge. It's equipped with a counterweight and anti-skate control to ensure proper tracking and prevent damage to the vinyl.
- CARTRIDGE: The cartridge is a critical component that houses the stylus (needle). It converts the physical movements of the stylus as it traces the vinyl grooves into an electrical audio signal.
- STYLUS (NEEDLE): The stylus is the needle that makes contact with the vinyl record's grooves. It's responsible for reading the audio information encoded on the record's surface.

Understanding these components and how they work together is fundamental to mastering the art of DJing with turntables. As you progress in your DJ journey, you'll appreciate the tactile nature and unique possibilities that turntables offer in shaping your DJing style.

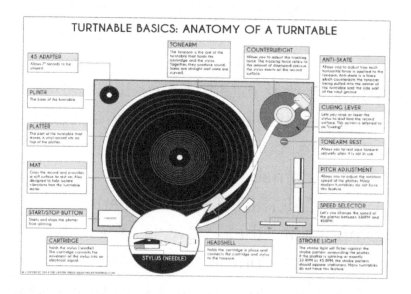

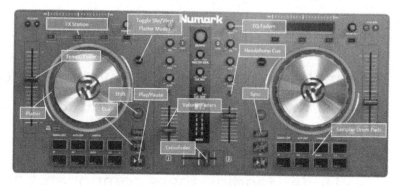

CDJs (Compact Disc Jockeys)

The role of CDJs in DJing and how they differ from turntables:

CDJs, short for Compact Disc Jockeys, are a type of DJ equipment commonly used by DJs, particularly in electronic dance music (EDM) and club environments. Understanding their role and how they compare to turntables is essential for aspiring DJs.

- *Role in DJing:* CDJs are digital media players designed for playing digital audio files from CDs, USB drives, or other digital storage media. They offer a more portable and convenient alternative to traditional vinyl turntables.
- *Key Differences from Turntables:*
- **Media Type:** CDJs use compact discs (CDs) or USB drives to store and play digital audio files, whereas turntables use vinyl records.
- **Pitch Control:** CDJs often feature pitch control to adjust the tempo of a track, similar to turntables, but with a digital interface.
- **Digital Display:** CDJs typically have digital displays that show track information, waveform displays, and other relevant data, providing DJs with visual cues.

- **Cue Points:** CDJs allow DJs to set cue points, which are specific points in a track that can be instantly jumped to during playback.
- **Looping:** CDJs offer looping capabilities, enabling DJs to repeat specific sections of a track seamlessly.

CDJ features, including pitch control, cue points, and looping:

CDJs come equipped with a range of features that enhance a DJ's performance and creativity.

- *Pitch Control:* CDJs feature pitch control sliders or buttons that allow DJs to adjust the tempo (speed) of a track. This is crucial for beatmatching and mixing tracks smoothly.
- *Cue Points:* DJs can set cue points at specific locations in a track. These cue points serve as markers, enabling quick navigation to desired sections of the track during a performance.
- *Looping:* CDJs provide loop functions that allow DJs to create seamless loops of a particular section of a track. This can be used creatively to

extend instrumental sections or build tension on the dancefloor.

• *Digital Displays:* Most CDJs come with digital displays that show track information, time elapsed, and a visual representation of the track's waveform. DJs use this information to make precise mixes and transitions.

How to use CDs and USB drives with CDJs for digital DJing:

CDJs offer flexibility when it comes to playing digital music from CDs or USB drives. Here's how to use these media with CDJs:

• *CDs:*
• Burn audio CDs with your desired tracks using CD burning software.
• Insert the CD into the CDJ's disc drive.

- Use the CDJ's controls to load and play tracks from the CD.
  - *USB Drives (Flash Drives):*
- Prepare a USB drive by organizing your digital music files into folders or playlists.
  - Insert the USB drive into the CDJ's USB port.
  - Navigate through your music library using the CDJ's interface and load tracks from the USB drive.

Using CDs and USB drives with CDJs provides DJs with a digital platform for DJing, offering the convenience of carrying a vast music library in a compact and portable format.

Mastering the use of CDJs opens up new possibilities for DJs, allowing them to harness digital technology while maintaining the tactile feel and performance aspects of DJing.

Controllers

DJ controllers and their place in modern DJ

setups:

DJ controllers have become an integral part of modern DJ setups, offering versatility and convenience to DJs of all skill levels.

- *Role in DJing:* DJ controllers are hardware devices that provide tactile control over DJ software, allowing DJs to manipulate and mix digital audio tracks. They are a bridge between traditional DJing with vinyl or CDs and the digital age.
- *Versatility:* Controllers are highly versatile and adaptable, making them suitable for various DJing styles and environments, from small home setups to large club performances.

Various types of DJ controllers, including all-in-one units and modular setups:

There are different types of DJ controllers to suit various preferences and needs:

- *All-in-One Controllers:* These are standalone units that combine all the essential components needed for DJing into a single device. They typically include jog wheels, mixer controls, performance pads, and built-in audio interfaces. All-in-one controllers are user-friendly and great for beginners.

• *Modular Controllers:* Modular setups allow DJs to customize their gear by using separate components for different functions. For example, you can use modular jog wheels, mixers, and performance pads connected to a central controller or computer. Modular setups provide greater flexibility but may require more advanced technical knowledge.

The functions and features of DJ controllers, including jog wheels, performance pads, and faders:

DJ controllers are equipped with a range of features that empower DJs to manipulate and mix digital music with precision and creativity.

• *Jog Wheels:* Jog wheels mimic the feel of vinyl turntables and are used for scratching, pitch bending, and cueing. They provide tactile control over track playback.

- *Performance Pads:* These are pressure-sensitive pads used for triggering samples, hot cues, loops, and effects. DJs can create dynamic performances by tapping or pressing these pads.
- *Faders:* Faders control the audio levels (volume) and EQ (equalization) of each track in a mix. They include channel faders for individual tracks and a crossfader for smooth transitions between tracks.
- *Knobs and Encoders:* Controllers often feature knobs and encoders that adjust parameters such as EQ settings, filter sweeps, and effect parameters. These controls offer fine-tuned adjustments.
- *Mixer Section:* DJ controllers typically include a mixer section with controls for adjusting channel levels, crossfading, and applying EQ. Some controllers offer more advanced mixer features like filter knobs and effects control.
- *Audio Interface:* Many DJ controllers come with built-in audio interfaces, allowing DJs to connect headphones and speakers directly to the controller. This simplifies setup and eliminates the need for external sound cards.

- *LCD Screens:* Some controllers feature built-in LCD screens that display track information, waveform visualizations, and other useful data, enhancing the DJ's workflow.

Understanding the functions and features of DJ controllers is essential for harnessing the full potential of these devices. Whether you're looking for the tactile feel of jog wheels or the versatility of performance pads, controllers offer a wide range of creative possibilities for DJs in the digital age.

Mixers

The central role of mixers in DJ setups and their functions:

Mixers are the heart of any DJ setup, allowing DJs to blend multiple audio sources, apply effects, and shape the sound to create seamless transitions and captivating performances.

- CENTRAL ROLE: Mixers serve as the central hub where various audio sources, such as turntables, CDJs, controllers, and microphones, are connected and manipulated before being sent to the sound system.
- FUNCTIONS: The primary functions of a DJ mixer include adjusting audio levels (volume control), equalization (EQ), crossfading between tracks, applying effects, and managing input sources.

Different types of mixers, such as two-channel and four-channel mixers:

Mixers come in various configurations, catering to different DJing styles and requirements:

- TWO-CHANNEL MIXERS: These mixers have two channels, typically used for mixing two audio sources simultaneously, such as two turntables or CDJs. Two-channel mixers are popular among scratch DJs and those who prefer simplicity.
- FOUR-CHANNEL MIXERS: Four-channel mixers provide additional flexibility by accommodating up to four audio sources. DJs can mix and transition between more tracks, making

them suitable for genres like house, techno, and EDM, where layering and blending multiple tracks are common.

Essential mixer features, including EQ, crossfaders, and effects sends:

Understanding the features and controls of a mixer is crucial for precise and creative DJing:

• EQ (EQUALIZATION): EQ controls allow DJs to adjust the frequency balance of each audio source. Common EQ controls include Low (bass), Mid (midrange), and High (treble). DJs use EQ to shape the sound and blend tracks harmoniously.

• CROSSFADER: The crossfader is a horizontal control that allows DJs to transition smoothly between two audio sources. It's often used for cutting and scratching. Crossfaders can be assigned to different channel pairs and adjusted for different crossfade curves.

• CHANNEL FADERS: Each channel on the mixer has its fader for adjusting the volume of that specific audio source. Channel faders are used for precise level control during mixing.

- CUE (PRE-FADER LISTEN): The cue feature allows DJs to listen to a channel's audio in their headphones before it's sent to the main sound system. This is essential for beatmatching and cueing tracks.

- EFFECTS SENDS: Many mixers include effects sends, which enable DJs to apply external effects processors to their audio sources. This can include delay, reverb, or other creative effects.

- MIC INPUT AND CONTROLS: Mixers often have a microphone input with controls for adjusting the microphone's volume, EQ, and effects send. This is useful for DJs who incorporate vocals or announcements into their performances.

- MASTER OUTPUT AND BOOTH OUTPUT: Mixers have master output controls for adjusting the overall volume sent to the main sound system. Some mixers also have booth output controls, allowing DJs to control the volume in the DJ booth or monitor speakers separately.

- HEADPHONE OUTPUT AND CUE CONTROLS: Mixers include a headphone output for monitoring the mix privately. DJs can use cue controls to select which channels they hear in their headphones.

- PHONO/LINE INPUTS: Mixers often feature both phono and line inputs to accommodate various audio sources, such as turntables, CDJs, and external devices.

Understanding these essential mixer features and controls empowers DJs to craft seamless mixes, perform creative transitions, and manipulate the sound to their liking. A DJ's choice of mixer and their mastery of its functions can greatly influence the quality and style of their performances.

Headphones

The importance of quality headphones for DJing:

Headphones are a critical tool for DJs, serving various purposes that are essential to the art of DJing.

- CUEING AND BEATMATCHING: DJs use headphones to preview upcoming tracks (cueing) and synchronize their beats (beatmatching) before introducing them to the main sound system. This ensures seamless transitions between tracks.

- ISOLATION: Quality headphones provide sound isolation, blocking external noise and allowing DJs to focus on the music in their headphones without interference from the venue's sound.

- MONITORING MIX: Headphones are used to monitor the mix as it's heard by the audience. DJs can make real-time adjustments to EQ, levels, and effects, ensuring the best possible sound quality for the audience.

The different types of headphones, including closed-back and on-ear models:

DJs have a choice of headphone types, each with its advantages and considerations:

- CLOSED-BACK HEADPHONES: Closed-back headphones have sealed ear cups, offering excellent sound isolation. They prevent sound leakage, making them ideal for DJing in noisy environments. Closed-back headphones tend to have a more pronounced bass response.

 • OPEN-BACK HEADPHONES: Open-back headphones have perforated ear cups that allow some sound to escape. They often have a more natural and spacious sound but provide less isolation. Open-back headphones are better suited for critical listening but may not be ideal for DJing in loud clubs.

 • ON-EAR VS. OVER-EAR: On-ear headphones rest on the ears, while over-ear headphones encircle the ears. Over-ear headphones generally provide better sound isolation and comfort for extended use, making them a popular choice among DJs.

Headphone features such as sound isolation and frequency response:

When choosing headphones for DJing, it's important to consider various features that affect their performance:

 • SOUND ISOLATION: Quality headphones offer effective sound isolation, reducing the impact of external noise. Closed-back and over-ear headphones tend to excel in this regard.

- FREQUENCY RESPONSE: The frequency response of headphones determines the range of frequencies they can reproduce. DJs often prefer headphones with a balanced frequency response that accurately reproduces bass, mids, and highs.

- DRIVER SIZE: The size of the headphone's driver affects its sound quality and bass response. Larger drivers can produce deeper bass, but they may be less portable.

- DURABILITY AND BUILD QUALITY: DJ headphones should be built to withstand the rigors of the road. Look for headphones with durable materials and robust construction.

- COMFORT AND FIT: Comfort is crucial for long DJ sessions. Consider headphones with padded ear cushions and an adjustable headband for a secure and comfortable fit.

- DETACHABLE CABLES: Headphones with detachable cables are more convenient for DJing, as you can replace damaged cables without replacing the entire headset.

- ROTATING EAR CUPS: Many DJ headphones have rotating ear cups, allowing for easy single-ear monitoring and convenient storage.

Choosing the right headphones for DJing is a personal decision that depends on your preferences and the specific demands of your DJing environment. Quality headphones are an investment that can significantly impact your performance and the quality of your mixes.

Speakers

The Significance of Speakers (PA Systems) in DJing:

Speakers, often referred to as PA (Public Address) systems, are indispensable tools in the world of DJing, serving several critical purposes:

- SOUND AMPLIFICATION: Speakers convert electrical audio signals from DJ equipment into audible sound that can be heard by the audience.

They are the final link in the audio chain, making the music come alive.

- SOUND QUALITY: The quality of the speakers directly impacts the quality of the sound. High-quality speakers can reproduce music accurately, capturing the nuances and details of the audio.

- VENUE COVERAGE: The choice of speakers and their placement within the venue determines how well the music is distributed throughout the space. Properly configured speaker systems ensure that every corner of the venue receives clear, consistent sound.

Speaker Configurations, Including Two-Way and Three-Way Systems:

Speaker configurations refer to the number of drivers (individual speaker components) and their respective roles in reproducing sound:

- TWO-WAY SYSTEMS: These speakers have two drivers – a woofer for handling low frequencies (bass and midrange) and a tweeter for high frequencies (treble). They are commonly used in smaller venues and DJ setups. Two-way speakers strike a balance between size and sound quality.

• THREE-WAY SYSTEMS: Three-way speakers add an additional driver, typically a midrange driver, to the woofer and tweeter. This configuration is capable of reproducing a broader range of frequencies with greater detail. Three-way systems are often employed in larger venues or for premium sound quality.

Power Ratings, Speaker Placement, and Considerations for Different Venues:

To effectively use speakers in DJing, it's essential to consider the following factors:

• POWER RATINGS: Speakers have power ratings that indicate their handling capacity. These ratings encompass RMS (continuous) power and peak power. DJs should ensure that their amplifiers and speakers are appropriately matched to avoid distortion or damage.

• SPEAKER PLACEMENT: The proper placement of speakers is crucial for achieving even sound distribution. Consider room acoustics, audience size, and the venue's layout when positioning speakers. Avoid placing speakers near reflective surfaces that can cause sound reflections or phase cancellation.

- ANGLES AND STACKING: Adjust the angles of speakers (tilting or angling them) to direct sound where it's needed, especially in venues with irregular shapes or multiple listening areas. For larger events, consider stacking speakers vertically to cover a broader area effectively.

- VENUE SIZE: The size of the venue dictates the power and quantity of speakers required. Smaller venues may only need a pair of powered speakers, while larger clubs or outdoor events may necessitate multiple speakers, subwoofers, and additional amplification.

- SUBWOOFERS: Subwoofers are specialized speakers designed to reproduce deep bass frequencies. DJs often use subwoofers to enhance the low-end impact of music in their setups. Proper subwoofer placement and integration are essential for achieving a balanced sound.

- SOUND CHECK: Before a performance, conduct a sound check to ensure that the sound system is set up correctly and that sound is balanced throughout the venue. Adjust EQ settings and speaker levels as needed.

Understanding the principles of speaker configurations, power ratings, placement, and venue considerations is paramount for DJs to provide an outstanding auditory experience for their audience. The choice and placement of speakers can significantly impact the success of a DJ performance.

Setting Up Your DJ Gear

Choosing the Right Location

Selecting the appropriate location for your DJ setup is a crucial initial step in ensuring a successful and enjoyable DJing experience. Here are some key considerations:

- SPACE: The available space in your chosen location is a critical factor. Ensure that there's enough room to accommodate your DJ equipment, including turntables, CDJs, controllers, mixers, and speakers. A clutter-free space allows for comfortable and safe operation.

- ELECTRICAL OUTLETS: Check for the availability and accessibility of electrical outlets in your chosen location. DJ equipment requires power, so it's essential to have enough outlets nearby to plug in all your gear. Consider using surge protectors or power strips to safely manage multiple devices.

- ACOUSTICS: The acoustics of the room can significantly affect the sound quality of your DJ setup. Rooms with hard surfaces, like wood or tile floors and bare walls, tend to create sound reflections and can lead to poor sound quality. Consider adding acoustic treatments such as rugs, curtains, or acoustic panels to improve sound absorption and reduce unwanted reflections.

- VENTILATION: DJ equipment can generate heat during extended use. Ensure that the chosen location has adequate ventilation to prevent overheating. Proper airflow helps maintain the optimal performance and longevity of your gear.

- ACCESSIBILITY: Think about the ease of access to your DJ setup. Make sure you can reach all your equipment comfortably without straining or tripping over cables. Accessibility is essential for smooth DJing and quick adjustments during your performance.

- LIGHTING: Adequate lighting is essential for operating your DJ equipment, especially in dimly lit environments. Consider adding adjustable lighting fixtures or LED lights to illuminate your setup and create a visually appealing atmosphere.

- CABLE MANAGEMENT: Plan for cable management to keep your setup organized and avoid tripping hazards. Use cable clips, ties, or cable channels to route and secure cables neatly.

- SOUND ISOLATION: If you're DJing in a shared living space or an area where noise might be a concern, consider soundproofing or sound isolation measures. This can include adding rugs, curtains, or acoustic panels to minimize sound leakage.

- PERSONAL COMFORT: Lastly, consider your own comfort while DJing. Ensure that your setup location allows you to maintain a good posture and offers a clear view of your equipment and the audience (if applicable). Comfortable DJing enhances your performance and enjoyment.

Choosing the right location for your DJ setup is a crucial step that sets the stage for your DJing experience. It impacts both the functionality and the aesthetics of your setup. By carefully considering factors like space, electrical outlets, acoustics, and comfort, you can create an ideal environment for your DJing sessions and performances.

Assembling Your DJ Setup

Assembling your DJ setup correctly is crucial for a smooth and successful DJing experience. Here are step-by-step instructions for setting up your DJ equipment:

1. **Positioning Your DJ Gear:**
   - Place your turntables, CDJs, or DJ controller on a stable surface, such as a DJ booth, table, or dedicated DJ stand. Ensure that the surface is level to prevent your equipment from wobbling during your performance.

- Position your mixer adjacent to your DJ gear. The mixer acts as the central hub for connecting your audio sources and adjusting sound levels.

- Arrange your speakers at an appropriate distance from your setup. Position them at ear level and ensure they are facing the audience for optimal sound distribution.

2. Connecting Your DJ Equipment:

- Connect your turntables, CDJs, or DJ controller to the appropriate channels on your mixer. Use RCA or XLR cables for audio connections, ensuring that the left and right channels are correctly connected.

- If you're using a microphone, connect it to the microphone input on the mixer.

- Use the mixer's outputs to connect to your amplifier or powered speakers. Ensure that the connections match the type of outputs on your mixer (e.g., XLR, TRS, or RCA).

- If you're using headphones, connect them to the headphone output on the mixer.

3. Powering Your Equipment:

- Plug your DJ equipment and mixer into electrical outlets using the appropriate power cables. Use surge protectors or power strips if needed to manage multiple devices.

- Power on your DJ gear and mixer. Verify that all devices are receiving power and functioning correctly.

4. **Setting Mixer Levels and EQ:**

- Adjust the channel gain or trim controls on your mixer to set the appropriate input levels for your DJ equipment. Avoid clipping or distorting audio signals by keeping levels in the green or yellow range.

- Use the mixer's EQ controls to fine-tune the sound. Typically, you have Low (bass), Mid (midrange), and High (treble) controls. Adjust these to achieve a balanced mix.

5. **Testing Audio:**

- Cue up a track and use your headphones to monitor it. Ensure that the audio is clear and that you can hear both channels (left and right) correctly.

- Check that the sound from your speakers is balanced and free from distortion. Make any necessary adjustments to the mixer or DJ gear settings.

Cable Management Tips:

Proper cable management keeps your DJ setup organized, minimizes tripping hazards, and ensures the longevity of your cables. Here are some cable management tips:

• Use cable clips, ties, or Velcro straps to bundle and secure cables neatly.

• Label your cables with tags or color-coding to easily identify them.

• Avoid running cables across walkways or areas where people might trip over them. Use cable channels or tape to secure cables to the floor if necessary.

• Create a dedicated cable routing path to keep cables organized and prevent tangling.

• Regularly inspect your cables for wear and tear, and replace damaged cables promptly to maintain signal quality.

By following these step-by-step instructions and implementing proper cable management techniques, you can assemble your DJ setup efficiently, minimize technical issues, and ensure a safe and organized workspace for your DJing sessions and performances.

Powering On and Off

Safely powering on and off your DJ gear is essential to prevent damage and ensure a smooth start to your DJing sessions. Here are the steps for both processes:

Powering On:

Verify Connections: Before powering on your DJ gear, double-check that all audio and power connections are properly set up and secure. Ensure that no cables are loose or disconnected.

Start with the Mixer: If you're using separate DJ equipment components (turntables, CDJs, controllers, mixer, etc.), begin by turning on your mixer or the central hub of your setup. This ensures that your audio signals are properly routed.

Power Up the DJ Equipment: Turn on your individual DJ equipment components one by one. Start with your turntables, CDJs, or controller. Allow each device a few seconds to initialize before proceeding to the next.

Check for Errors: While your gear powers up, keep an eye on any LED displays or indicators for error messages or unusual behavior. If you notice any issues, consult your gear's user manual or troubleshoot as needed.

Wait for Initialization: Some DJ equipment may require a brief initialization period after powering on. Be patient and wait until all equipment is ready for use.

Test Audio and Functionality: Once your gear is powered on, test the audio output and functionality. Use headphones to cue up a track and check that both left and right channels are working correctly.

Powering Off:

Prepare for Shutdown: Before powering off your DJ gear, ensure that your audio sources are paused or stopped, and the volume on your mixer is set to minimum.

Turn Down Volume: On your mixer, gradually lower the channel faders and master volume to zero. This prevents sudden audio spikes and potential damage to your speakers or hearing.

Power Off DJ Equipment: Turn off your DJ equipment components in the reverse order in which you powered them on. Start with your turntables, CDJs, or controller, and proceed to your mixer and any other devices.

Power Off Amplifiers and Speakers: If you're using external amplifiers and passive speakers, turn off the amplifiers before shutting down your DJ gear. This prevents audio pops and potential speaker damage.

Disconnect Power: Once all equipment is powered off, disconnect the power cables from the electrical outlets. This not only conserves energy but also reduces the risk of electrical issues.

Secure Cables: After disconnecting the power, secure and organize your cables to prevent tangling or tripping hazards.

By following these steps for powering on and off your DJ gear, you can help prevent damage, maintain the longevity of your equipment, and ensure a smooth and hassle-free start to your DJing sessions. Properly powering down your gear also contributes to a safe and organized workspace.

Understanding Audio Cables

Types of Audio Cables

In DJ setups, various types of audio cables are used to connect and transmit audio signals between different components of your setup. Understanding the purpose and usage of each type of cable is essential for setting up and configuring your DJ gear correctly. Here are some common audio cables used in DJing:

RCA Cables (Phono Cables)

- **Purpose:** RCA cables are widely used for connecting audio sources like turntables, CDJs, controllers, and other DJ equipment to mixers, amplifiers, and speakers.
- **Usage:** RCA cables typically come in pairs, with red and white connectors. The red connector represents the right audio channel, while the white connector represents the left channel. These cables transmit unbalanced audio signals.

XLR Cables:

- **Purpose:** XLR cables are used for connecting microphones, mixers, and powered speakers in DJ setups, providing balanced audio signals with high-quality sound transmission and noise rejection.
- **Usage:** XLR cables have three pins and are commonly used for microphones and professional audio equipment. They are known for their secure and reliable connections and are often used for longer cable runs.

1/4-inch TRS Cables (Tip-Ring-Sleeve):

- **Purpose:** 1/4-inch TRS cables are versatile and used in various DJ applications, including connecting headphones, balanced outputs from DJ mixers, and instruments like synthesizers.

- **Usage:** TRS cables have a tip (T), ring (R), and sleeve (S) connector. They can transmit both balanced and unbalanced audio signals, making them suitable for various DJ gear connections.

1/8-inch (3.5mm) TRS Cables (Mini-Jack Cables):

- **Purpose:** 1/8-inch TRS cables are used for connecting smaller devices like smartphones, laptops, and portable media players to mixers, controllers, or headphone outputs.

- **Usage:** These cables have a 3.5mm plug on one end (commonly found on headphones and portable devices) and a 1/4-inch or 1/8-inch plug on the other end, depending on the device it's connecting to.

USB Cables:

- **Purpose:** USB cables are used to connect DJ controllers, sound cards, and MIDI controllers to computers or other compatible devices.

- **Usage:** USB cables transmit both data and power, making them essential for communication between DJ software and hardware controllers. They come in various shapes and sizes, depending on the specific devices.

Ethernet (RJ45) Cables:

- **Purpose:** Ethernet cables are used for connecting networking-enabled DJ equipment, such as digital mixers, to networks or other compatible devices for remote control and data sharing.
- **Usage:** Ethernet cables use standardized RJ45 connectors and can transmit digital audio and control data between devices over local area networks (LANs).

Understanding the types and purposes of these audio cables is crucial for setting up your DJ equipment correctly and ensuring reliable audio connections in your DJing setup. Proper cable selection and organization are essential for delivering high-quality sound and seamless performances.

Cable Connections

Correctly Connecting Audio Cables:

Properly connecting audio cables is essential to ensure optimal audio quality and prevent damage to your equipment. Here are steps to follow when connecting audio cables:

Check Compatibility: Ensure that the connectors on both ends of the cable match the input/output ports on your equipment. For example, use RCA cables for RCA connectors, XLR cables for XLR connectors, and so on.

Turn Off Equipment: Before connecting or disconnecting cables, make sure your DJ equipment is powered off. This reduces the risk of electrical damage and audio spikes.

Secure Connections: Gently insert the connectors into the respective jacks until they click or fit snugly. Ensure a firm but not excessive connection. Tighten any threaded connectors, such as XLR or 1/4-inch TRS, by turning them clockwise.

Color Coding: Pay attention to color-coded connectors when using stereo (dual-channel) audio cables, such as RCA or 1/4-inch TRS. Match the red connector to the right channel and the white or black connector to the left channel.

Organize Cables: Keep cables organized and untangled to prevent interference and tripping hazards. Consider using cable clips, ties, or channels to manage and secure your cables.

Correctly Disconnecting Audio Cables:

Safely disconnecting audio cables is just as important as connecting them:

Turn Off Equipment: Always power off your DJ equipment before disconnecting any cables.

Hold the Connector: When removing a cable, grasp the connector firmly near the jack and pull it straight out gently. Avoid pulling on the cable itself, as this can damage the connectors or the cable.

Use Care with Locking Connectors: Connectors like XLR and Speakon may have locking mechanisms. To disconnect them, press or release the locking mechanism before pulling the connector out.

Tips for Troubleshooting Common Cable-Related Issues:

Even with proper cable connections, issues may still arise. Here are some troubleshooting tips for common cable-related problems:

Check for Loose Connections: Occasionally, connectors can become loose over time. Inspect all cable connections and tighten them as needed.

Swap Cables: If you suspect a faulty cable, try swapping it with a known-working cable to determine if the issue is cable-related.

Inspect for Damage: Examine cables for physical damage, including cuts, kinks, or exposed wires. Damaged cables should be replaced.

Eliminate Interference: If you hear unwanted noise or interference, ensure that audio cables are separated from power cables and other sources of electromagnetic interference.

Test One Component at a Time: If you're experiencing audio problems, isolate the issue by testing each component in your setup separately. This helps pinpoint the source of the problem.

Use Quality Cables: Invest in high-quality audio cables to minimize signal loss and interference. Cheap or damaged cables can significantly impact sound quality.

Clean Connectors: Occasionally, connectors may accumulate dirt or corrosion. Use a contact cleaner or isopropyl alcohol on a clean cloth to gently clean connectors.

By following these guidelines for connecting and disconnecting audio cables and using troubleshooting techniques, you can maintain optimal audio quality, prevent equipment damage, and address common cable-related issues that may arise during your DJing sessions.

Chapter 2: Music Essentials

This chapter will provide aspiring DJs with the knowledge and skills they need to build and manage a diverse music library, organize their tracks effectively, understand essential musical elements like BPM and key, and prepare playlists and setlists for engaging DJ performances. Additionally, it explores the historical context of different music formats and the transition to digital DJing.

Building Your Music Library

A well-curated and diverse music library is the foundation of DJing. It's not just about having a vast collection; it's about having the right tracks for the right moment. In this section, we'll explore the importance of a diverse music library, tips for sourcing and acquiring music, and how to organize your collection effectively.

The Importance of a Diverse Music Library in DJing:

Musical Variety: A diverse library allows you to cater to a wide range of musical tastes and preferences. It empowers you to adapt to different audiences and settings, from clubs to weddings and corporate events.

Creative Freedom: A rich music collection gives you creative freedom. You can experiment with different genres, eras, and styles to craft unique and memorable DJ sets.

Professionalism: Having a diverse and well-organized library demonstrates professionalism to your clients and audience. It shows that you are prepared for any request or situation.

Tips for Sourcing and Acquiring Music

Purchase Music Legally: Support artists and the music industry by purchasing tracks legally. Buy your music from reputable online stores, such as Beatport, iTunes, Bandcamp, or Juno Download. Look for high-quality, lossless formats like WAV or FLAC.

Subscribe to DJ Record Pools: DJ record pools are subscription-based services that provide DJs with a regular selection of new music. These pools often offer DJ-friendly edits and remixes. Examples include BPM Supreme, DJCity, and ZipDJ.

Explore Streaming Services: Streaming platforms like Spotify, Tidal, and Apple Music can be valuable for music discovery. Create playlists and save tracks you might want to add to your collection. Keep in mind that not all streaming services provide DJ-ready audio quality, so you may need to purchase high-quality versions of your chosen tracks.

Dig for Vinyl and CDs: If you're interested in vinyl or CD DJing, consider visiting record shops, thrift stores, or online marketplaces to find physical copies of music. Vinyl records can provide a unique tactile experience and access to tracks not available digitally.

Networking with Fellow DJs: Connect with other DJs in your community or online. Sharing music recommendations and tracks with fellow DJs can be an excellent way to discover hidden gems.

Organizing Your Music Collection for Easy Access

Use Descriptive File Names: When you download or rip music, use file names that include relevant information, such as the artist, track title, and remix version. This makes it easier to identify tracks at a glance.

Tag Your Tracks: Add metadata tags to your music files, including artist name, track title, genre, BPM, and key. Many DJ software applications can read and use this metadata for better organization and mixing.

Create Folders and Subfolders: Organize your music into folders and subfolders based on genres, moods, or occasions. Having a well-structured directory system can significantly speed up your track selection process.

Create Playlists: Build playlists for specific gigs, themes, or genres. Playlists help you prepare and execute your DJ sets more efficiently.

Backup Your Library: Regularly back up your music library to prevent data loss. Use external hard drives, cloud storage, or redundant storage solutions for added security.

Building a diverse music library takes time and effort, but it's a crucial investment for your DJing career. By following these tips and organizing your collection effectively, you'll have the right music at your fingertips for any DJing opportunity that comes your way.

Organizing Your Music

Organizing your music library is essential for efficient music selection and seamless DJing. Here are some best practices and techniques to help you structure, categorize, and label your tracks effectively:

Folder Structure

Creating a logical folder structure is the foundation of organizing your music library. Here are some best practices:

- **Genre-Based Folders:** Organize your music into genre-specific folders. This makes it easier to find tracks when you're planning your sets.

- **Subfolders:** Within genre folders, create subfolders for sub-genres or themes. For example, if you have a "House" genre folder, you can have subfolders for "Deep House," "Tech House," and so on.
- **Date-Based Folders:** Consider creating folders for specific time periods or years if you have a vast collection spanning different eras.
- **Special Occasion Folders:** Create folders for special occasions or recurring events like weddings, holidays, or club residencies.

Metadata and Tagging

Adding metadata and tags to your tracks is crucial for quick and efficient music selection. Here's how to label your tracks effectively:

- **Artist and Title:** Ensure that the artist name and track title are accurately labeled. This basic information should be consistent and error-free.
- **Genre:** Assign a genre tag to each track. This allows you to filter and search for tracks by genre, making it easier to build genre-specific sets.

- **BPM (Beats Per Minute):** Tag each track with its BPM value. This is crucial for beatmatching and creating smooth transitions between songs.
- **Key:** Include key information using the Camelot Wheel notation (e.g., 3A, 8B). Knowing the key helps with harmonic mixing and creating harmonic transitions.
- **Remix Version:** Specify if a track is an original mix, remix, or extended version. This helps you choose the most suitable version for your set.
- **Release Year:** Tag tracks with their release year. This can be useful when you want to create themed sets or explore music from a specific era.
- **Comments:** Use the comments field for additional notes or information about a track, such as its energy level, mood, or any specific mixing techniques you plan to use.

Playlists and Setlists

Creating playlists and setlists is an excellent way to organize your music for specific gigs or occasions:

- **Create Themed Playlists:** Build playlists for different themes or moods, such as "Chillout," "Peak Time," or "Summer Vibes."

- **Setlists:** For live DJ performances, create setlists that outline the tracks you plan to play in a specific order. This helps you prepare and stay organized during your sets.

- **Smart Playlists:** Some DJ software allows you to create smart playlists that automatically populate based on criteria like BPM, key, or genre. Utilize these to keep your playlists up to date.

Regular Maintenance

Maintaining your organized music library is an ongoing process:

- **Delete Unwanted Tracks:** Periodically review your collection and remove tracks that you no longer need or enjoy. This helps keep your library streamlined.

- **Update Metadata:** Correct any incorrect or missing metadata as you come across it. Consistently maintaining your metadata ensures accurate organization.

- **Backup Your Library:** Regularly back up your music library to prevent data loss. Consider using cloud storage, external hard drives, or network-attached storage (NAS) for redundancy.

Effective organization not only saves you time but also enhances your DJing experience. With a well-structured library, you can focus on creativity and seamless mixing during your performances.

Understanding BPM and Key

BPM (Beats Per Minute) and musical key are fundamental concepts in DJing. They play a crucial role in creating smooth and harmonically pleasing mixes. In this section, we'll explain BPM and its significance in DJing, delve into harmonic mixing and the importance of key compatibility, and discuss tools and software for analyzing BPM and key information.

Explaining BPM (Beats Per Minute) and Its Significance in DJing

BPM (Beats Per Minute) is a measure of tempo, representing the number of beats (or pulses) in music occurring within one minute. BPM is a fundamental element in DJing for several reasons:

Beatmatching: DJs use BPM to match the tempo of two tracks to create seamless transitions. This involves adjusting the playback speed of one track to align its beats with the beats of another track.

Creating Energy: BPM can influence the energy level of a DJ set. Tracks with higher BPMs often feel more energetic and suitable for peak moments, while lower BPMs can create a more relaxed or chilled vibe.

Transitions: Smooth transitions between tracks are achieved by ensuring their BPMs are closely matched. This prevents abrupt tempo changes that can disrupt the dancefloor's flow.

Mixing Styles: Different DJing styles, such as house, techno, and drum and bass, are often characterized by specific BPM ranges. Knowing the typical BPM range for a genre helps DJs select appropriate tracks.

Harmonic Mixing and the Importance of Key Compatibility

Harmonic mixing is the practice of mixing tracks that are harmonically compatible, meaning they share compatible musical keys. The musical key of a track represents its tonal center and scale. Harmonic mixing is significant for several reasons:

Smooth Transitions: Harmonically compatible tracks blend together more smoothly, creating harmonious and pleasing transitions. Incompatible keys can clash and create dissonance.

Emotional Impact: Mixing harmonically can enhance the emotional impact of your DJ sets. Tracks in the same or related keys can reinforce the mood you're trying to convey.

Key Mixing: DJs often mix in key, meaning they select tracks with keys that are harmonically related. For example, mixing a track in the key of C major with one in G major is a common key mixing practice.

Tools and Software for Analyzing BPM and Key Information:

To assist DJs in analyzing BPM and key information, various tools and software are available:

- **DJ Software:** Most modern DJ software applications display the BPM of tracks in your library. Some also provide key analysis tools that automatically detect the musical key of each track.
- **Key Detection Software:** Dedicated key detection software, such as Mixed In Key and Camelot Wheel, can analyze the key of your tracks and provide harmonic compatibility information.
- **DJ Controllers:** Many DJ controllers have built-in BPM and key display screens, allowing you to see this information while performing.
- **Mobile Apps:** There are mobile apps designed for DJs that can analyze BPM and key on the go. These apps often use your device's microphone to detect BPM.

Understanding BPM and key, and their significance in DJing, allows you to create more engaging and harmonically pleasing DJ sets. By selecting tracks with compatible BPMs and keys and using the right tools for analysis, you can elevate your DJ performances and provide a more enjoyable experience for your audience.

Creating Playlists and Setlists

Creating playlists and setlists is a crucial part of DJ preparation. Playlists help you organize your music library for different occasions, while setlists are essential for planning and executing live DJ performances. Here are some tips and considerations for building playlists and setlists effectively:

Building Playlists

Genre-Based Playlists: Organize your music into playlists based on genres or sub-genres. For example, you can have playlists for "House," "Techno," "Hip-Hop," "Indie Rock," and so on. This makes it easy to find tracks that match the style of your event.

Mood and Energy Level: Create playlists that reflect different moods or energy levels. For example, you can have playlists for "Chillout," "Peak Time," "Sunset Vibes," or "Late-Night Grooves." This allows you to tailor your music to the atmosphere of the moment.

Occasion-Specific Playlists: Build playlists for specific occasions or themes, such as "Summer BBQ," "Holiday Party," or "90s Throwback." These playlists can help you curate the perfect soundtrack for special events.

Collaborative Playlists: Consider creating collaborative playlists on platforms like Spotify, where friends or event organizers can contribute their song requests or suggestions.

Regular Updates: Keep your playlists up to date by adding new tracks and removing outdated ones. A fresh playlist ensures that your music is relevant and exciting.

Constructing Setlists for Live DJ Performances

Plan Your Journey: When creating a setlist for a live performance, think of it as a musical journey. Consider how you want to start, build energy, and eventually bring it down. Plan your transitions accordingly.

Know Your Audience: Understand the preferences of your audience and the type of event you're playing. Are they expecting a specific genre or vibe? Are there any requests or must-play tracks?

Balance Crowd Favorites: Include crowd-pleasers and well-known tracks in your setlist to engage the audience. These familiar tunes can create moments of excitement and connection.

Experiment and Surprise: Don't be afraid to introduce lesser-known or unique tracks into your setlist. Surprise your audience with unexpected gems that showcase your musical taste and expertise.

Practice Your Setlist: Practice your setlist multiple times before your performance. This helps you become familiar with the flow of your set and the transitions between tracks.

Backup Tracks: Have backup tracks ready in case you need to adapt to the crowd's response or unforeseen technical issues. Flexibility is key in live DJing.

Record Your Setlists: Consider recording your live sets for review and analysis. This can help you refine your track selection and performance techniques.

Remember that creating playlists and setlists is both an art and a science. While organization and planning are essential, spontaneity and adaptability also play a significant role in successful DJ performances. Balancing crowd favorites with your own musical identity is a key aspect of creating memorable DJ sets.

Music Formats - Vinyl, CDs, and Digital

The world of DJing has seen a significant evolution in music formats over the years. DJs have transitioned from vinyl records to CDs and, more recently, to digital audio files. Each format has its unique characteristics, advantages, and drawbacks. In this section, we'll explore the evolution of these music formats, discuss the pros and cons of each, and provide insights into transitioning from analog to digital DJing.

Evolution of Music Formats in DJ Culture:

Vinyl Records: Vinyl records were the foundation of DJ culture. DJs used turntables and vinyl records to mix and manipulate music. This format offered tactile control and a unique sound quality, contributing to the birth of hip-hop, house, and techno music.

CDs (Compact Discs): With the advent of digital technology, CDs became the next format of choice for DJs. CDs offered better sound quality than vinyl and were more durable. CDJs (Compact Disc Jockeys) emerged as specialized DJ equipment.

Digital Audio Files: The digital revolution transformed DJing. DJs began to use digital audio files (e.g., MP3s) stored on laptops or USB drives. DJ software and controllers allowed for greater flexibility, track management, and real-time effects.

Pros and Cons of Each Music Format

Vinyl Records:

- **Pros:**
- Unique tactile experience with vinyl manipulation.
  - Warm and distinct analog sound.
  - Collectible and nostalgic value.
  - **Cons:**
  - Bulky and heavy to transport.
  - Limited track selection per record.
  - Prone to wear and tear.

CDs (Compact Discs):

- **Pros:**
- Better sound quality than vinyl.
- More durable and portable than vinyl.
- Track selection and cue points.
- **Cons:**
- Still physical media, susceptible to damage.

- Limited track selection compared to digital.

Digital Audio Files:

- **Pros:**
- Vast music library at your fingertips.
- Easy to organize, search, and manage tracks.
- Instant access to cue points and effects.
- Seamless integration with DJ software and controllers.
- **Cons:**
- Loss of tactile vinyl experience.
- Dependent on technology and power sources.
- Potential for file compatibility issues.

Transitioning from Analog to Digital DJing

Transitioning from analog (vinyl or CDs) to digital DJing can be a smooth process with some considerations:

Equipment Choice: Invest in digital DJ

equipment such as controllers, CDJs, or turntables with digital capabilities. Choose hardware and software that suit your DJing style and budget.

Digital Music Library: Build and organize a digital music library. Convert your vinyl or CD collection to digital formats or start acquiring digital tracks.

Software Proficiency: Familiarize yourself with DJ software. Learn how to organize your library, set cue points, and use effects.

Controller Mapping: If you're using DJ controllers, customize and map them to your preferences for a seamless transition.

Practice and Adaptation: Spend time practicing your digital DJing skills. Embrace the new possibilities and creative tools that digital DJing offers.

Backup and Redundancy: Have backup equipment and music sources in case of technical issues during performances.

Whether you choose vinyl, CDs, or digital, each format has its place in DJ culture. Many modern DJs incorporate elements from all three formats to create unique and dynamic performances, demonstrating the ongoing evolution and innovation in the world of DJing.

Chapter 3: DJing Techniques

This section covers the fundamental DJing techniques that every DJ should master. These techniques are essential for creating seamless mixes, engaging the audience, and expressing your unique style as a DJ. Here are the key DJing techniques to be discussed:

Beatmatching

Beatmatching is the foundation of DJing. It involves aligning the beats (rhythmic pulses) of two tracks so that they play in sync. This technique ensures smooth transitions between songs and is essential for maintaining a consistent dancefloor groove.

Beatmatching Basics

- **What Are Beats?** Beats are the rhythmic pulses in music that give it its sense of timing and groove. In most electronic dance music, these beats are steady and repetitive, making them ideal for beatmatching.
- **Two Tracks:** Beatmatching involves aligning the beats of two tracks, typically the one currently playing (playing deck) and the one you want to mix in (cue deck).
- **Pitch Control:** DJs use the pitch control on their equipment (turntables, CDJs, or software) to adjust the speed (BPM) of one of the tracks until the beats of both tracks are perfectly synchronized.

Tips for Beatmatching

Listen Carefully: Train your ears to detect the beats in music accurately. Practice counting beats and sub-dividing them into smaller intervals, like half-beats or quarter-beats.

Use Headphones: When beatmatching, use headphones to cue the incoming track (cue deck). This allows you to hear the beats and make adjustments without the audience hearing the process.

Adjust Pitch Control: Gently adjust the pitch control of the cue deck until the beats of both tracks are aligned. Increase the pitch to speed up the track and decrease it to slow it down.

Sync Phases: Pay attention to the phrasing of both tracks. Ensure that significant elements like the kick drum or snare drum hit together for a tight mix.

Beatmatching Software: Some DJ software and controllers have features like sync buttons that can help with beatmatching. While these can be useful, it's essential to learn the manual beatmatching technique to understand the fundamentals.

Practice with Metronomes: To refine your beatmatching skills, practice alongside a metronome. This can help you develop a strong sense of timing.

Develop Muscle Memory: Beatmatching requires coordination between your hands (for pitch control) and your ears (for listening). Over time, this coordination becomes intuitive, and you develop muscle memory.

Stay Patient: Beatmatching can be challenging for beginners, but with practice, it becomes second nature. Don't get discouraged if it takes time to master.

Record Your Mixes: Recording your DJ sets and analyzing them afterward can help you identify areas where your beatmatching can be improved.

Experiment: Once you've mastered basic beatmatching, experiment with creative variations, like pitch play or pitch bending, to add your unique style to your mixes.

Remember that beatmatching is a foundational skill that opens the door to more advanced DJing techniques. It's the key to creating seamless transitions and maintaining a consistent dancefloor groove, making it an essential skill for any DJ.

Phrasing And Structure

Phrasing is a fundamental concept in DJing that goes hand in hand with beatmatching and smooth mixing. It involves understanding the structure of musical compositions and recognizing when phrases begin and end. Mastering phrasing allows DJs to create seamless transitions and maintain the flow and energy of their sets. Here's a more detailed explanation of phrasing and tips for DJs:

Understanding Musical Phrasing

- **Phrases Defined:** In music, a phrase is a self-contained musical unit that often consists of a specific number of bars or measures. These phrases are like building blocks that make up the structure of a track.

- **Phrases in DJing:** DJs should pay attention to phrases in songs they're mixing. A phrase can be as short as four bars or extend to eight, sixteen, or more bars, depending on the genre and style of the music.

- **Phrasing Elements:** Phrases often have characteristic elements, such as an introduction, buildup, drop, breakdown, and outro. These elements contribute to the overall musical narrative of a track.

Tips for DJs on Phrasing

Listen Actively: Train your ears to actively listen for changes in musical elements that signal the start or end of a phrase. These elements may include variations in melody, rhythm, or instrumentation.

Count Bars: Develop the habit of counting bars or measures in the music you're mixing. This helps you keep track of the song's structure and anticipate phrase changes.

Cue Points: Set cue points or hot cues at significant moments within a track, such as the beginning of a new phrase or the start of a drop. This allows you to easily jump to these points during your mixes.

Practice Phrasing Transitions: Experiment with transitioning between tracks at specific phrase changes. For example, you can start mixing in a new track at the beginning of a breakdown in the outgoing track for a smooth transition.

Phrasing Alignment: When beatmatching, ensure that the beats and phrases of both tracks align correctly. This prevents awkward or jarring transitions that can occur if phrases are misaligned.

Energy Management: Understanding phrasing helps you manage the energy of your DJ sets. You can build anticipation during the buildup phase and create excitement during the drop or climax.

Visual Aids: Some DJ software and controllers provide visual aids that display the waveform and highlight the structure of a track, making it easier to identify phrases.

Record and Analyze Sets: Record your DJ sets and analyze them later. Pay attention to how you handled phrasing transitions and where improvements can be made.

Experiment with Phrasing Styles: Different genres and styles of music may have unique phrasing patterns. Experiment with various styles to diversify your DJing skills.

Recognizing and mastering phrasing is essential for DJs aiming to create fluid and engaging mixes. It allows you to tell a musical story, maintain the dancefloor's energy, and keep your audience captivated throughout your sets.

Mixing

Mixing is a core skill that defines the art of DJing. It's the process of seamlessly transitioning from one track to another, creating a continuous and engaging musical experience. DJs use various techniques, including blending, cutting, and dropping, to mix tracks together. Here's a deeper look at mixing techniques and tips for mastering them:

Mixing Techniques

Blending: Blending, or beatmatching, involves smoothly transitioning from one track to another by matching their beats and gradually adjusting the crossfader or mixer's volume controls. This technique creates a seamless and harmonious mix. DJs often use headphones to cue the incoming track before blending it in.

Cutting: Cutting is a more abrupt mixing technique where the DJ quickly switches from one track to another, typically at a significant point like a drop or chorus. This technique can create a sudden burst of energy and excitement.

Dropping: Dropping involves introducing a new track suddenly and dramatically. It's often used to surprise the audience or to change the direction and intensity of the music abruptly. DJs can use this technique for building tension and delivering climactic moments.

Filtering and EQ: DJs use equalization (EQ) and filter effects to manipulate the frequency balance of tracks. By selectively boosting or cutting bass, midrange, and treble frequencies, DJs can create smooth transitions and creative sound shaping during mixes.

FX and Effects: DJ software and controllers often come with a range of effects like reverb, delay, flanger, and more. These effects can be applied to tracks during transitions to add depth, texture, and creativity to the mix.

Tips for Mastering Mixing

Practice Beatmatching: Beatmatching is the foundation of mixing. Practice aligning the beats of two tracks until it becomes second nature. Train your ears to detect when the beats are perfectly synced.

Use Headphones: Invest in quality DJ headphones and use them to cue and monitor tracks. This helps you beatmatch accurately and avoid unwanted sounds in the mix.

Know Your Tracks: Familiarize yourself with your music library. Understand the structure, arrangement, and phrasing of tracks so you can plan your mixes effectively.

Plan Transitions: Think ahead and plan how you want to transition from one track to another. Consider factors like energy level, key compatibility, and phrasing to create smooth transitions.

Master Your Equipment: Learn the ins and outs of your DJ equipment, whether it's turntables, CDJs, controllers, or software. Familiarity with your gear enables you to execute your mixing techniques with precision.

Record and Analyze Mixes: Record your DJ sets and listen to them critically. Analyze your transitions, timing, and technique to identify areas for improvement.

Experiment: Don't be afraid to experiment with different mixing techniques and effects. Developing a unique mixing style sets you apart as a DJ.

Read the Crowd: Pay attention to the audience's reaction and energy level. Adjust your mixing style and track selection accordingly to keep the dancefloor engaged.

Stay Smooth: Keep your mixing transitions smooth and avoid harsh or jarring changes that can disrupt the flow of the music.

Practice Regularly: Practice consistently to refine your mixing skills. The more you practice, the more confident and capable you'll become as a DJ.

Mixing is both an art and a technical skill. It's a DJ's way of storytelling through music, creating an emotional journey for the audience. With dedication, practice, and creativity, you can master mixing techniques and deliver dynamic and memorable DJ sets.

EQ and Effects

Equalization (EQing) is a vital tool in a DJ's

arsenal for shaping the sound and creating seamless transitions between tracks. It involves adjusting the balance of frequencies—bass, midrange, and treble— to achieve a harmonious mix. Here's a more in-depth look at EQing and how DJs use it effectively:

Understanding Equalization

- **Frequency Bands:** An EQ typically consists of three main frequency bands:
- **Bass:** This controls the low-frequency sounds, including the kick drum and bassline.
- **Midrange:** This affects the mid-frequency range, which includes vocals, synths, and instruments like guitars.
- **Treble:** This manages the high-frequency elements, including hi-hats, cymbals, and snares.
- **Cut and Boost:** EQs allow DJs to either cut (reduce) or boost (increase) the intensity of specific frequency bands. Cutting frequencies removes unwanted elements, while boosting emphasizes certain aspects of a track.

Using EQ in DJing

Smooth Transitions: DJs use EQ to make transitions between tracks smoother. For example, you can gradually reduce the bass on the outgoing track while increasing the bass on the incoming track to seamlessly introduce the new song.

Eliminate Clashes: EQ helps prevent frequency clashes between tracks. If two tracks have clashing basslines or vocals, you can use EQ to reduce the conflicting frequencies, allowing both tracks to coexist harmoniously.

Creating Builds: During build-ups in a mix, you can gradually boost the treble or midrange frequencies to build anticipation and energy. This technique adds excitement before a drop.

Filtering: DJs often use filter effects, a type of EQ, to manipulate the sound. A low-pass filter reduces high frequencies, creating a muffled or distant effect, while a high-pass filter reduces low frequencies, creating a more subdued sound.

Mixing In Key: EQ can be used to mix tracks in key. For example, if you're transitioning from one track in the key of C major to another in G major, you can use EQ to gradually adjust the frequencies to match, creating a harmonious mix.

Sound Shaping: EQing can shape the sound to suit the DJ's style or the mood of the moment. For example, cutting the bass and boosting the treble can create a brighter, more energetic sound.

Tips for Effective EQing

Practice A/B Testing: Experiment with EQ settings and listen to the impact on the sound. Try different cuts and boosts to understand how they affect the tracks.

Use EQ Sparingly: Avoid excessive EQing, which can result in unnatural or unpleasant sound. Make subtle adjustments to maintain the integrity of the tracks.

Know Your Tracks: Familiarize yourself with your music library to know which frequencies are prominent in each track. This helps you make informed EQ decisions.

Pay Attention to Phrasing: Consider the phrasing of tracks when applying EQ. Make changes at logical points in the music to avoid disrupting the flow.

Record and Analyze Mixes: Record your DJ sets and review them to evaluate your EQing techniques. This helps you refine your skills and develop a better ear for sound shaping.

Experiment and Be Creative: Don't be afraid to experiment with EQ settings and create unique soundscapes that reflect your personal style as a DJ.

Mastering EQing is essential for DJs to achieve a balanced and harmonious mix. It allows you to control the sound, create smooth transitions, and tailor the music to the atmosphere of the moment, enhancing your DJing skills and creativity.

Using Effects is a creative aspect of DJing that allows you to add unique textures, depth, and atmospheres to your mixes. Effects processors, whether built into your DJ software or available through external hardware, offer a wide range of possibilities to enhance your sets. Here's an overview of some common DJ effects and tips on how to use them effectively:

Common DJ Effects

Reverb: Reverb adds a sense of space and depth to your mix. It simulates the reflection of sound in a physical environment, creating a natural or ethereal ambiance. Use reverb to give tracks a sense of space or to transition between songs smoothly.

Delay: Delay repeats the audio signal with a time delay, creating an echo effect. It's often used to add depth and rhythmic complexity to tracks. You can use delay to create build-ups, accentuate drops, or add subtle echoes to vocals.

Flanger: Flanger produces a sweeping, swirling effect by modulating the audio signal's phase. It's known for its distinctive "jet plane" sound. DJs use flanger to add motion and excitement to tracks or for creative transitions.

Filter: Filters shape the frequency content of a track. High-pass filters remove low frequencies, while low-pass filters remove high frequencies. DJs use filters to create build-ups, drops, or to emphasize specific frequency ranges.

Phaser: Phaser creates a sweeping, swirling effect similar to flanger but with a different tonal quality. It's often used to add texture and movement to tracks or to create unique transitions.

Bitcrusher: Bitcrusher reduces the audio resolution, creating a "crushed" or lo-fi sound. DJs use bitcrusher to add a retro or gritty feel to tracks or for creative sound mangling.

Pitch Shift: Pitch shifting allows you to change the pitch of a track in real-time. This effect can be used for harmonic mixing, creating vocal variations, or adding a surreal quality to the mix.

Tips for Using Effects Effectively

Know Your Effects: Familiarize yourself with the effects available in your DJ software or hardware. Understand how each effect works and its sonic characteristics.

Practice Control: Develop precise control over effect parameters, such as wet/dry mix, depth, rate, and resonance. Practice using effects in time with the music to create seamless transitions.

Subtlety Is Key: Effects should enhance the music, not overpower it. Use effects sparingly and with purpose to avoid overwhelming the mix.

Sync to the Beat: Many DJ software and controllers offer sync options to align effects with the beat. This helps maintain rhythmic coherence.

Plan Your Moments: Identify specific moments in your DJ sets where effects can add impact or creativity. These moments could include breakdowns, drops, or transitions.

Record and Analyze: Record your sets and analyze how you used effects. This helps you refine your techniques and develop your unique style.

Experiment: Don't be afraid to experiment with unconventional effects combinations or to create your own signature effects patterns.

Listen Actively: Pay close attention to the effect's impact on the sound. Train your ears to discern when an effect complements the mix and when it might be excessive.

Using effects in DJing is a creative process that allows you to shape and elevate your mixes. With practice and experimentation, you can develop a keen sense of when and how to apply effects to create unique soundscapes and enhance your DJ sets.

Advanced Mixing Techniques

Track Selection is a critical aspect of DJing that can significantly impact the success of your DJ sets. The art of choosing the right tracks involves understanding the mood, energy level, and musical compatibility of songs to create a coherent and memorable performance. Here are some key considerations and tips for effective track selection:

Key Considerations for Track Selection

Audience and Venue: Consider the preferences of your audience and the type of venue or event you're playing. Different crowds have varying musical tastes, and the vibe of a venue can influence your track selection.

Set Goals: Determine the goals of your DJ set. Are you aiming to create a high-energy dancefloor, set a chill mood, or take the audience on a musical journey? Your track selection should align with your objectives.

Mood and Energy: Tracks evoke different emotions and energy levels. Be mindful of the mood you want to convey and the energy you want to maintain throughout your set.

Musical Compatibility: Ensure that the tracks you select are musically compatible. Consider factors like musical key, tempo, and genre when choosing songs that flow seamlessly together.

Build and Release: Plan the progression of your set. Start with tracks that set the tone and gradually build energy. Use climactic tracks for peak moments and consider moments of relief or introspection.

Balance Familiarity: Include familiar and crowd-pleasing tracks in your set to engage the audience. However, don't rely solely on popular hits. Incorporate lesser-known gems to showcase your musical depth.

Surprises and Creativity: Introduce surprises and unexpected tracks to keep the audience engaged. Creative selections can make your set stand out.

Musical Diversity: Mix up your track selection with a variety of sounds, styles, and eras. This keeps your set fresh and dynamic.

Tips for Effective Track Selection

Know Your Music: Spend time exploring and getting to know your music library. Understand the characteristics of each track, including BPM, key, and mood.

Create Playlists: Organize your tracks into playlists based on genre, mood, or energy level. Having pre-arranged playlists makes it easier to find the right track at the right time.

Use Cue Points: Set cue points in your tracks to mark key moments like drops, breakdowns, or transitions. This allows for precise mixing and timing.

Read the Crowd: Pay attention to the audience's reaction. Adapt your track selection based on their energy and engagement.

Practice Mixing: Practice mixing different tracks together to ensure they work well in a live setting. Experiment with transitions to find what works best.

Record and Analyze Sets: Record your DJ sets and analyze them to evaluate the effectiveness of your track selection. Identify moments that worked well and areas for improvement.

Stay Current: Stay updated with new music releases in your preferred genres. Incorporate fresh tracks into your sets to keep them relevant.

Trust Your Instincts: Ultimately, trust your instincts as a DJ. Your intuition and musical taste play a significant role in track selection.

Track selection is an art that evolves with experience. As you gain more DJing experience and exposure to different audiences, you'll refine your track selection skills and develop a unique style that resonates with your audience.

Advanced mixing techniques are essential for DJs who want to elevate their skills and create more dynamic and captivating sets. These techniques go beyond basic beatmatching and blending and allow DJs to craft intricate and innovative mixes. Here are some advanced mixing techniques to explore:

Phrasing and Timing: Understanding musical phrasing and timing is crucial for advanced mixing. Tracks are typically divided into phrases, and DJs should learn to recognize these divisions and transition between tracks at the right moments for seamless mixing.

Harmonic Mixing: Harmonic mixing involves mixing tracks that are harmonically compatible. This technique enhances the musicality of your sets by ensuring that tracks with similar keys blend smoothly. To achieve harmonic mixing, use key detection software to analyze the key of your tracks and select harmonically compatible songs to mix.

Multi-Deck Mixing: If you're using a setup with multiple decks or controllers, explore the art of mixing three or more tracks simultaneously. This advanced technique allows for more intricate layering and creative possibilities. However, it requires precise timing and a deep understanding of the tracks you're working with.

Layering and Looping: Layering involves playing two or more tracks simultaneously, often with one track serving as a background layer while another takes the foreground. Looping allows you to repeat specific sections of a track to create tension or build energy. Experiment with layering and looping to create intricate and engaging mixes.

EQ Automation: While basic EQing involves adjusting the low, mid, and high frequencies of tracks, advanced DJs use EQ automation to create dynamic and evolving mixes. By automating EQ adjustments throughout a mix, you can gradually transform the sound and take the audience on a sonic journey.

Filter and FX Manipulation: DJ mixers often come with built-in filters and effects processors. Advanced DJs use these tools to manipulate the sound in real-time. Filters can be used to create dramatic build-ups and drops, while effects like reverb, delay, and flanger can add texture and creativity to your sets.

Scratching and Turntablism: If you haven't already explored scratching and turntablism, these advanced techniques can add flair and creativity to your sets. Scratching involves manipulating the sound of a track by moving a vinyl record back and forth against a stylus. Turntablism includes various techniques like beat juggling and scratching that require precision and practice.

Cue Point Triggering: Take advantage of cue points and hot cues to trigger specific parts of a track at precise moments. This technique allows for quick and creative transitions and can be especially useful for genre-bending and mashup-style sets.

Sample Triggering: Triggering samples and loops in real-time is another advanced technique that can add depth and complexity to your mixes. Experiment with sample pads or controllers to incorporate vocal snippets, sound effects, or percussion elements into your sets.

Reversed Mixing: Reverse mixing involves playing a track backward or in reverse. When done tastefully, it can create surprising and unique transitions. However, this technique should be used sparingly and with consideration for the audience's reaction.

Remember that mastering advanced mixing techniques takes time and practice. It's essential to experiment and push your boundaries while maintaining a strong connection with your audience and the energy of the dancefloor. With dedication and creativity, you can develop a signature style and take your DJing to new heights.

Chapter 4: Scratching and Turntablism

Scratching

Scratching is a unique and expressive turntablism technique that involves manipulating the sound of a track by moving a vinyl record back and forth against a stylus. While not essential for all DJing styles, scratching can add flair, creativity, and a distinct personality to your DJ sets. Here's an overview of scratching and some tips for incorporating it into your performances:

Understanding Scratching

- **Origin:** Scratching originated in the early days of hip-hop and turntablism, with DJs using vinyl records and turntables to create rhythmic and percussive sound effects by manipulating the records.

- **Technique:** Scratching involves moving a vinyl record in various directions (forward, backward, circular motions) against the stylus while the turntable is in motion. This action creates distinctive sound patterns, including stabs, chirps, flares, and transforms.

- **Control:** Scratching requires precise hand-eye coordination and control. DJs use one hand to manipulate the record while the other controls the crossfader to manage the sound's on/off effect.

Tips for Incorporating Scratching

Learn the Basics: Start by mastering basic scratching techniques like the baby scratch and forward scratch. These foundational scratches help you develop control and timing.

Practice, Practice, Practice: Scratching is a skill that takes time and dedication to perfect. Regular practice sessions are essential for improving your scratching abilities.

Study Turntablism: Study the techniques and styles of renowned turntablists to gain inspiration and insights. Learn from tutorials, videos, and online communities dedicated to scratching and turntablism.

Use the Right Equipment: Invest in high-quality turntables, cartridges, and needles. The right equipment can make a significant difference in your scratching performance.

Understand Musical Phrasing: Scratching is not just about making random sounds. Understand the musical phrasing of the tracks you're scratching over and use that knowledge to create rhythmic and melodic patterns.

Practice with a Metronome: Scratching in time with a metronome or a beat can help you develop a tight sense of rhythm and precision.

Incorporate Scratching Sparingly: While scratching can be a crowd-pleaser, it's essential to use it strategically. Introduce scratching during climactic moments in your set or to add excitement and variation.

Combine with Other Techniques: Scratching works well when combined with other DJing techniques like beatmatching, mixing, and effects. Experiment with how scratching can enhance your transitions and overall performance.

Record and Review: Record your scratching sessions and DJ sets to assess your progress. This allows you to identify areas for improvement and track your development as a turntablist.

Be Creative: Scratching is a form of self-expression. Don't be afraid to experiment and develop your unique scratching style. Push the boundaries of what you can do with the technique.

Scratching and turntablism are advanced DJing techniques that can elevate your skills and set you apart as a DJ. Here's a comprehensive guide to mastering these skills, from the basics to more advanced techniques:

Basic Scratching Techniques

Baby Scratch: The baby scratch is the foundation of scratching. Start by moving the record back and forth while hitting the crossfader's "open" and "closed" positions. Practice maintaining a consistent rhythm and clean sound.

Forward Scratch: In a forward scratch, move the record forward (away from you) while hitting the crossfader. This creates a sound similar to the baby scratch but with a different motion.

Transform: The transform is a fast and rhythmic scratch. Execute multiple forward scratches in quick succession while opening and closing the crossfader rapidly. This creates a "choppy" and percussive effect.

Chirp: The chirp is a combination of a forward scratch and the crossfader. Move the record forward while closing the crossfader and then quickly open it. This produces a "chirping" sound.

Intermediate Scratching Techniques

Crab Scratch: The crab scratch is an advanced scratch that uses all of your fingers to manipulate the crossfader. Each finger controls a different position of the crossfader, allowing for intricate and rapid scratching patterns.

Flare: The flare scratch involves using both hands to manipulate the record and crossfader. One hand controls the record movement while the other hand manipulates the crossfader. This technique allows for complex and continuous patterns.

Twiddle/Orbit: The twiddle, also known as the orbit, is a circular scratch motion. Move the record in a circular pattern while manipulating the crossfader to create a swirling sound effect.

Crab Flare Combo: Combine elements of the crab and flare scratches to create intricate and dynamic scratch patterns. This technique requires precise coordination between both hands and fingers.

Advanced Turntablism Techniques

Juggling: Juggling involves manipulating multiple copies of the same record to create complex and seamless patterns. DJs can "juggle" between different copies of a record to create intricate routines.

Body Tricks: Turntablists use body tricks to manipulate the record and crossfader by touching them with various parts of their body, such as the chin, elbow, or nose. These techniques add a visual and creative element to scratching.

Beat Juggling: Beat juggling involves manipulating two records to create seamless and rhythmic patterns. DJs cut and manipulate beats from two records to create new rhythms and grooves.

Word Play: Some turntablists incorporate vocal samples, words, or phrases into their scratching routines. This adds a storytelling element and allows DJs to "speak" through their scratches.

Tips for Mastering Scratching and Turntablism:

Practice Regularly: Scratching and turntablism require consistent practice to develop precision and speed. Dedicate time to daily or weekly practice sessions.

Use Quality Equipment: Invest in high-quality turntables, cartridges, and needles for optimal scratching performance.

Watch Tutorials: Study tutorials, videos, and performances by experienced turntablists to learn new techniques and gain inspiration.

Experiment: Don't be afraid to experiment with different scratch patterns, combinations, and rhythms. Creativity is key in turntablism.

Record Your Scratches: Record your scratching sessions to assess your progress and identify areas for improvement.

Join Turntablist Communities: Connect with other turntablists and DJs through online forums, social media, and local DJ communities. Sharing ideas and experiences can be invaluable.

Collaborate: Collaborate with other musicians and DJs to incorporate scratching into live performances and studio recordings.

Scratching is a dynamic and artistic aspect of DJing that can set you apart from others and add a personal touch to your performances. Whether you're a turntablist or simply want to incorporate scratching into your DJ sets occasionally, honing your scratching skills can be a rewarding journey.

Building A Set

Planning and Set Structure are key elements of effective DJing. A well-structured DJ set involves careful planning of the flow, energy, and emotional journey you want to take your audience on. Here's a breakdown of the planning and set structuring process, along with some tips for creating engaging DJ sets:

Understanding Set Structure:

Opening: The opening of your set sets the tone and establishes the initial mood. It's an opportunity to draw the audience in and create anticipation.

Build-Up: After the opening, gradually build energy by selecting tracks that are slightly more energetic than the previous ones. The build-up should increase the crowd's excitement and anticipation.

Climax: The climax is the high-energy peak of your set. This is where you drop your most energetic tracks, create intense moments, and get the crowd dancing and cheering.

Transitions: Between each phase (opening, build-up, climax), use smooth transitions to maintain the flow and keep the audience engaged.

Variation: Include moments of variation within your set to keep it interesting. This can involve introducing different genres, styles, or even surprising the audience with unexpected tracks or remixes.

Emotional Range: Plan to take the audience on an emotional journey. Incorporate tracks with various emotional qualities, from euphoric and uplifting to more introspective or groovy.

Cool Down: Towards the end of your set, gradually lower the energy by selecting tracks that are slightly less intense. This allows the crowd to catch their breath and wind down.

Closing: The closing of your set should leave a lasting impression. Choose a memorable track or combination of tracks that send the audience off with a positive and lasting experience.

Tips for Planning and Structuring Your DJ Sets

Know Your Audience: Understand the preferences and energy levels of your audience. Tailor your set to match their expectations.

Know Your Music: Familiarize yourself with your music library so that you can choose tracks that fit seamlessly into your set structure.

Create Playlists: Organize your music into playlists or folders that correspond to different phases of your set structure. This makes it easy to find the right tracks when you need them.

Practice Your Set: Rehearse your set multiple times to ensure a smooth flow and perfect transitions. This also helps you become more confident in your track selection.

Record Your Sets: Record your DJ sets and analyze them. Listen for areas where you can improve the structure, transitions, and energy flow.

Be Flexible: While planning is essential, be prepared to adjust your set on the fly based on the crowd's response. Flexibility allows you to respond to the energy of the moment.

Build a Story: Think of your set as a musical story. Craft a narrative that takes the audience on a journey and keeps them engaged.

Set Goals: Consider what you want to achieve with your set. Whether it's creating a high-energy dance party or providing a laid-back lounge atmosphere, your goals will inform your set structure.

Record Your Ideas: Keep a record of track combinations, transitions, and creative ideas that work well in your sets. This can serve as a reference for future performances.

Stay Inspired: Stay inspired by exploring new music, attending other DJs' performances, and seeking fresh ideas for set structures.

Effective planning and set structuring are essential for creating engaging and memorable DJ sets. By carefully considering the flow, energy, and emotional journey of your performance, you can craft sets that captivate and entertain your audience from start to finish.

Performance Techniques are creative elements that go beyond technical DJing skills and can add excitement, uniqueness, and a personal touch to your sets. These techniques allow you to express your creativity and connect with your audience on a deeper level. Here are some performance techniques you can incorporate into your DJ sets:

Looping: Looping involves selecting a specific section of a track and repeating it to create a continuous and rhythmic pattern. You can loop drum beats, melodies, vocals, or any other part of a song to build tension or extend a groove. Experiment with different loop lengths and combinations to add variation to your sets.

Cue Juggling: Cue juggling is a technique where you rapidly switch between cue points to create rhythmic and percussive patterns. It involves using the cue buttons on your DJ controller or software to trigger short snippets of a track. This technique can add a dynamic and playful element to your sets, especially during breakdowns or transitions.

Live Remixing: Live remixing allows you to reinterpret and reshape tracks on the fly. You can use effects, filters, and EQ to manipulate the sound of a track, creating unique remixes that are exclusive to your set. Live remixing can be particularly effective during climactic moments to surprise and captivate the audience.

Mashups and Bootlegs: Create mashups or bootlegs by combining elements from two or more tracks to create a new and exciting blend. This technique allows you to showcase your creativity and surprise the audience with unexpected combinations.

Sample Triggering: Use a sampler or sample pads to trigger short audio samples, sound effects, or vocal snippets during your sets. These samples can add texture, humor, or thematic elements to your performance.

Scratching and Turntablism: As mentioned earlier, scratching and turntablism techniques can be powerful performance tools. Incorporate scratches, cuts, and transforms to showcase your skills and create engaging moments in your sets.

Layering Tracks: Layering involves playing multiple tracks simultaneously to create unique textures and harmonies. Careful selection of tracks and precise mixing can lead to mesmerizing sonic landscapes.

FX and Sound Design: Experiment with audio effects to shape the sound of your tracks. Use reverb, delay, filters, and other effects to create spatial and tonal changes that enhance the atmosphere of your sets.

Visual Effects and Lighting: Consider incorporating visual effects and lighting elements that synchronize with your music. Visuals can enhance the overall experience and create a multisensory journey for your audience.

Interactive Elements: Engage with your audience by taking requests, encouraging crowd participation, or integrating interactive elements like live visuals or social media interactions.

Thematic Sets: Design sets around specific themes, genres, or concepts. This can create a cohesive and immersive experience for the audience.

Emotional Storytelling: Craft your sets to tell a musical story or convey a particular emotion. Use track selection and mixing techniques to create a narrative arc that resonates with the audience.

Remember that while these performance techniques can add depth and excitement to your sets, it's essential to balance them with your technical DJing skills and track selection. The key is to use these techniques purposefully and in a way that enhances the overall experience for your audience. Experiment, practice, and find your unique style as a DJ performer.

Mastering these DJing techniques takes practice, dedication, and creativity. Whether you're a beginner or an experienced DJ, continually honing your skills in these areas will elevate your performances and make you a more versatile and dynamic   DJ.

Chapter 5: Reading the Crowd

Reading the Crowd is a crucial skill for DJs, as it allows you to connect with your audience, understand their preferences, and tailor your music selection and performance to create the perfect atmosphere for any event. Here's a comprehensive guide on how to effectively read the crowd and enhance your DJing skills:

Observe Body Language

- Pay attention to the body language of the audience. Are they dancing energetically, nodding their heads, or swaying to the music? These signs indicate a positive response to the current track.
- Watch for cues like smiles, clapping, or raised hands, which suggest that the crowd is enjoying the music.
- Conversely, be aware of signs of disinterest, such as people leaving the dancefloor or looking

disengaged. This may indicate that the current track or style isn't resonating with the audience.

Engage with Eye Contact

- Make eye contact with the audience, especially those closest to the DJ booth. This connection can help you gauge their reactions and energy levels.
- If you see someone enthusiastically enjoying a particular track, consider playing more in that style or tempo to maintain the positive vibe.

Interact Verbally

- Use the microphone (if available) to communicate with the audience. You can announce track titles, give shoutouts, and encourage crowd participation.
- Ask the audience how they're feeling or if they're ready for the next track. Their responses can guide your song selection.

Take Requests (Judiciously)

• Consider taking song requests from the crowd, but use your judgment. Ensure that the requested track aligns with the overall vibe and style of your set.

• Politely decline requests that don't fit the current mood or genre. Explain that you'll try to incorporate similar tracks if possible.

Adapt Your Set

• Be prepared to change your set on the fly based on the audience's reactions. If you notice a shift in energy or mood, adjust your track selection accordingly.

• If the crowd is responding well to a particular genre or style, explore similar tracks and build upon that momentum.

Mix in Real-Time

- DJing isn't just about track selection; it's about mixing and blending songs seamlessly. Mix tracks in real-time to maintain a continuous flow and keep the dancefloor engaged.
- Use mixing techniques like beatmatching, EQing, and transitions to create smooth and harmonious transitions between songs.

Balance Familiarity and Discovery

- Strive for a balance between playing familiar crowd-pleasers and introducing new or lesser-known tracks. This keeps the audience engaged while showcasing your musical depth.
- Surprise the crowd with creative transitions, mashups, or remixes to pique their interest.

Be Adaptable

- Be flexible and open to change. Not every track will resonate with every crowd, so have a diverse music library and be ready to switch gears if needed.

Maintain Energy Levels

- Manage the energy levels of your set effectively. Build anticipation, create peak moments, and provide occasional breaks to ensure the crowd's energy remains balanced.
- Pay attention to the overall arc of your set, including the opening, climax, and closing moments.

Record and Reflect

- Record your DJ sets and listen to them afterward. Analyze your performance to identify which tracks and transitions worked well and which areas could be improved.

Connect with Promoters and Event Organizers

- Build relationships with promoters and event organizers to gain insights into the expectations and preferences of the specific event you're DJing at. They may have valuable information about the target audience.

Trust Your Instincts

• While reading the crowd is essential, trust your instincts and musical intuition as a DJ. Your unique style and musical taste are valuable assets.

Reading the crowd is a skill that improves with experience. The more you DJ in diverse settings and for different audiences, the better you'll become at understanding and satisfying the crowd's musical desires.

Chapter 6: Performance Tips

As a DJ, your performance is not just about playing music; it's about engaging your audience, creating memorable experiences, and building your unique DJ persona. Here are some performance tips to help you excel in your DJing journey:

Developing Your DJ Persona

As a DJ, your performance is not just about playing music; it's about engaging your audience, creating memorable experiences, and building your unique DJ persona. Here are some performance tips to help you excel in your DJing journey:

Find Your Style: Your unique style sets you apart. This encompasses various elements:
Stage Name: Choose a stage name that reflects your identity and the kind of music you play.

Music Style: Define the style of music you want to be known for. This could be a specific genre or a combination of genres.

Appearance: Your look, including clothing and any visual elements in your setup, should be consistent with your style.

Show Confidence: Confidence is a magnet. When you're confident in your DJing skills, it radiates to your audience. It's not just about what you play but also how you present it.

Interact with the Crowd: Engaging with your audience is an essential part of DJing. This interaction can set the tone for your performance. Making eye contact, smiling, and responding to the crowd's energy can help establish a connection.

Stage Presence: Your stage presence encompasses how you physically perform while DJing. Consider your movements, gestures, and enthusiasm. An engaging stage presence can enhance your performance and captivate your audience.

Evolve Over Time: As you gain experience and refine your style, be open to growth and change.

DJing is an art that can evolve over time. Embrace new ideas, experiment with your style, and continually adapt to stay fresh and relevant.

Remember that your DJ persona is a key part of your brand and image. It can create a lasting impression on your audience and help you stand out in a competitive DJing landscape. Be true to yourself and your style, and let your personality shine through your performances.

Mixing with Confidence

Practice: Confidence often comes from competence. Dedicate time to practice your mixing and scratching skills regularly. The more you practice, the more confident you'll become.

Know Your Music: Familiarity with your music library is crucial. Know your tracks inside and out, including their BPMs, key, and structure. This knowledge will help you mix seamlessly and make quick decisions during your sets.

Prepare Your Set: Plan your set in advance by selecting tracks and organizing them in a playlist or folder. Having a well-structured set plan can boost your confidence, as you'll know what to play next.

Visualize Success: Before your performance, take a moment to visualize yourself succeeding. Imagine the crowd responding positively to your music, and picture yourself confidently mixing and performing.

Dress the Part: Your appearance can impact your confidence. Choose an outfit that makes you feel comfortable and represents your DJ persona. Confidence often starts with feeling good about how you look.

Learn from Mistakes: Understand that mistakes are a part of DJing. Even experienced DJs make errors from time to time. Instead of dwelling on mistakes, use them as learning opportunities to improve your skills.

Stay Calm Under Pressure: In high-pressure situations, such as technical issues or a less-responsive crowd, stay calm and composed. Your ability to handle adversity gracefully can boost your confidence and earn the respect of the audience.

Engage with the Crowd: Interacting with the audience can boost your confidence. Make eye contact, smile, and engage with the crowd. Their positive reactions can fuel your self-assurance.

Dealing with Mistakes

Stay Calm: If you make a mistake during your set, stay calm. Panicking can make the situation worse. Remember that most of the audience may not even notice minor mistakes.

Quick Recovery: If possible, make a quick recovery. Use effects, loops, or cues to get back on track. Experienced DJs can turn mistakes into creative moments.

Learn from Errors: After your set, take time to reflect on what went wrong and how you can prevent similar mistakes in the future. Continuous improvement is a key part of DJing.

Accept Imperfections: Understand that nobody is perfect. Imperfections can make your performances more human and relatable.

Creating Smooth Transitions

Practice Beatmatching: Beatmatching is the foundation of smooth transitions. Master the art of aligning the beats of two tracks so they play in sync.

Use EQ: Equalization (EQ) is essential for creating smooth transitions. Adjust the bass, midrange, and treble to achieve a balanced mix and make seamless transitions.

Plan Your Set: Prepare your set in advance and organize your tracks logically. This makes it easier to transition smoothly from one track to another.

Cue Points: Set cue points in your tracks to jump to specific sections instantly. This helps maintain the flow of your set.

Learn to Phrase: Understanding musical phrasing is crucial. Transition between tracks at the right moments to create seamless mixes.

Mixing Techniques: Explore different mixing techniques like blending, cutting, and dropping. Each technique offers a unique way to transition between tracks.

Using Effects: Effects processors can enhance your transitions. Experiment with effects like reverb and delay to create interesting transitions between songs.

With practice and experience, you can develop confidence, refine your DJ persona, handle mistakes gracefully, and create smooth transitions that keep your audience dancing all night. Remember that DJing is not just about playing music but about creating an unforgettable experience for your audience.

Chapter 7: DJ Gear Maintenance

Maintaining your DJ gear is essential to ensure reliable performance and longevity. Here's a comprehensive guide on DJ gear maintenance, covering cleaning and care, troubleshooting common issues, upgrading your equipment, and having backup gear:

Cleaning and Care

Proper cleaning and care of your DJ equipment are essential to ensure it performs reliably and has a long lifespan. Here are some tips for cleaning and caring for your gear:

1. Regular Cleaning Routine:

• Establish a routine for cleaning your gear. Depending on your usage, this may be after each gig, weekly, or monthly. Regular cleaning prevents dust and debris from accumulating and causing problems.

2. Unplug and Power Off:

• Always unplug your equipment and power it off before cleaning. This reduces the risk of electrical shocks and damage.

3. Use the Right Cleaning Tools:

• Invest in cleaning tools designed for electronic equipment. These may include soft, lint-free microfiber cloths, compressed air cans, and specialized cleaning solutions.

4. Cleaning Turntables and CDJs:

• Clean the platters or jog wheels with a soft cloth to remove dust and debris.
• Use compressed air to blow out dust from tight spaces and crevices.

• Clean the tonearm, cartridge, and stylus with a soft brush or stylus brush. Be gentle to avoid damage.

• Wipe down the exterior with a damp, lint-free cloth.

• Consider using a stylus cleaner or cleaning solution for the needle.

5. Cleaning Mixers:

• Use compressed air to remove dust from faders, knobs, and switches.

• Clean faders and knobs with a non-abrasive electronic cleaner or contact cleaner to prevent crackling or static noises.

• Wipe down the mixer's exterior with a damp, lint-free cloth.

6. Cleaning Controllers:

• Keep jog wheels, faders, and buttons clean and free from dirt or spills.

• Use compressed air to remove dust from tight spaces and crevices.

- Clean touch-sensitive pads and buttons with a damp cloth or specialized electronic cleaner.

7. Cleaning Headphones:

- Regularly clean the ear cushions and headband with a damp cloth to remove sweat and dirt.
- Ensure cables are free from knots or tangles and inspect them for damage.
- Store your headphones in a protective case when not in use to prevent damage.

8. Cleaning Speakers:

- Dust speaker cones and grilles regularly to maintain sound quality.
- Clean speaker cables and connectors to prevent interference or static noise.
- Protect speakers from moisture and extreme temperatures to prevent damage.

9. Cable Management:

- Keep your cables organized and free from knots to prevent damage and ensure reliable connections. Consider using cable ties or organizers.

10. Preventative Maintenance:

- Inspect your equipment for loose screws, loose connectors, or worn parts. Address any issues promptly to prevent further damage.

11. Storage:

- When not in use, store your gear in a clean, dry, and dust-free environment. Cover your equipment to protect it from dust and potential spills.

12. Professional Maintenance:

- Consider having your gear professionally serviced or calibrated periodically, especially if you rely on it for important performances.

13. Record Keeping:

• Maintain records of your gear's maintenance and any repairs. This documentation can be valuable if you need to reference previous servicing.

14. Transport Cases and Covers:

• Invest in high-quality transport cases and covers for your gear, especially if you travel frequently. These protective cases can shield your equipment from damage during transit.

By following these cleaning and care guidelines, you can help ensure your DJ equipment remains in top condition, performs reliably, and continues to deliver the best possible sound quality. Proper maintenance is a key part of being a responsible DJ and protecting your valuable gear investment.

Maintaining your turntables and CDJs is essential for smooth and high-quality performances. Here's a detailed guide on how to care for these components:

Turntables

1. Platters and Slipmats:

- Regularly clean the platters and slipmats to prevent dust buildup, which can affect turntable performance.
- Use a soft, lint-free cloth to wipe down the platters and slipmats, removing any dust and debris.
- If you use slipmats, clean them separately according to the manufacturer's instructions, as materials and care requirements may vary.

2. Tonearm and Cartridge:

- Clean and align your turntable's tonearm and cartridge regularly to ensure optimal sound quality.
- Use a stylus brush or soft brush to remove dust and debris from the stylus (needle).
- Check the alignment of your cartridge and adjust it if necessary, following the manufacturer's guidelines.
- Lubricate the tonearm bearings as recommended by the manufacturer to maintain smooth movement.

3. Needles or Styli:

• Inspect and clean your needles or styli regularly to prevent groove damage and maintain sound quality.

• Use a stylus brush or a specialized stylus cleaner to gently remove dirt and debris from the needle.

• Replace worn or damaged needles promptly to avoid damaging your vinyl records.

CDJs

1. Jog Wheels:

• Keep CDJ jog wheels clean to ensure smooth operation during scratching and cueing.

• Use a soft, lint-free cloth to wipe down the jog wheels and remove any dust or fingerprints.

• Avoid spilling liquids or substances on the jog wheels, as this can lead to sticky or unresponsive performance.

2. Exterior Cleaning:

- Wipe down the exterior of your CDJs with a soft, lint-free cloth to remove dust and fingerprints.
- Avoid using abrasive cleaners or excessive moisture when cleaning to prevent damage to the surface.

3. CD Slots and Discs:

- Periodically inspect the CD slots for debris or foreign objects that may interfere with loading and playback.
- Keep your CDs clean and free from scratches to prevent damage to the CDJ's laser lens and ensure accurate playback.

4. Firmware Updates:

- Check for firmware updates from the manufacturer and install them as recommended. Updated firmware can improve performance and fix bugs.

General Tips:

- Store your turntables and CDJs in a dust-free environment when not in use, and cover them with protective dust covers if possible.
- Avoid exposing your gear to extreme temperatures or direct sunlight, as this can damage components and affect performance.
- Use anti-static brushes or cloths to remove static buildup from your vinyl records and CD surfaces before playback.

Regular cleaning and maintenance of your turntables and CDJs will not only prolong their lifespan but also ensure that your DJ performances remain smooth and high-quality.

Troubleshooting Common Issues

Even with proper maintenance, issues may arise. Here are some common DJ gear problems and how to troubleshoot them:

Audio Distortion or No Sound

- Check your connections, including cables and plugs, for loose or damaged connections.
- Verify that your mixer's volume levels, EQ settings, and gain levels are correctly configured.
- Inspect your needles or stylus for damage or wear, and replace if necessary.

Skipping or Stuttering Playback

- Ensure your turntable platter or CDJ jog wheel is clean and free from dust or debris.
- Check the condition of your vinyl records or CDs for scratches or damage.
- Calibrate your turntable's tonearm or adjust the tracking force to the manufacturer's recommendations.

Non-Responsive Buttons or Knobs

- Clean buttons and knobs with electronic cleaner to remove dirt or debris.
- Check for loose or disconnected wires inside your gear.

• If the issue persists, consult the manufacturer's user manual or contact customer support for further assistance.

Upgrading Your Equipment

As your DJing skills progress, you may consider upgrading your gear to meet your evolving needs. Here are some considerations:

• Evaluate your current equipment and identify any limitations or areas where an upgrade would benefit your performance.
• Research new DJ gear models and features to determine which ones align with your goals and style.
• Set a budget and prioritize upgrades based on your specific needs and preferences.
• Before purchasing new gear, read reviews, watch video demonstrations, and seek recommendations from fellow DJs to make informed decisions.

Backup Gear

Having backup gear is crucial for ensuring

uninterrupted performances, especially during live gigs. Here's how to prepare and maintain backup equipment:

- Invest in backup headphones, cables, and adapters to address common issues on the fly.
- Carry a backup USB drive or CDs with your essential tracks in case of a computer or digital system failure.
- Regularly test and maintain your backup gear to ensure it's in working condition.
- Keep your backup gear organized and readily accessible during performances for quick swaps if needed.

By following these maintenance, troubleshooting, upgrading, and backup gear strategies, you can keep your DJ equipment in optimal condition and minimize disruptions during your performances. Maintaining and caring for your gear is an integral part of being a responsible and reliable DJ.

Chapter 8: Digital DJing and Software

Digital DJing has revolutionized the world of DJing, offering a wide range of creative possibilities and convenience. Here's an overview of digital DJing and software, including an introduction to DJ software, choosing the right DJ software, digital DJing techniques, and using MIDI controllers:

Introduction to DJ Software

DJ software is the heart and soul of modern DJing, offering a powerful platform for manipulating and mixing digital audio files with precision and creativity. Here are key points to understand about DJ software:

1. **Virtual Mixing Interface:** DJ software provides a virtual mixing interface on your computer or mobile device, mimicking the traditional setup of turntables and mixers. This interface allows you to

control and manipulate your music tracks with precision.

2. **Compatibility:** DJ software is versatile and compatible with various digital audio formats, including MP3, WAV, FLAC, and more. This versatility allows DJs to work with a vast library of music files.

3. **Core Features:** DJ software comes equipped with essential features that include:

- **Beatmatching:** DJ software helps you align the beats of two tracks to ensure they play in perfect sync, creating seamless transitions between songs.
- **Mixing:** You can smoothly transition from one track to another by adjusting volume levels, crossfader positions, and EQ settings.
- **Effects:** Most DJ software offers a range of built-in effects like reverb, delay, filters, and more, allowing you to add texture and creativity to your mixes.
- **Looping:** Create loops within tracks to extend sections, build tension, or create unique variations.
- **Cue Points:** Set cue points in your tracks, allowing you to quickly jump to specific sections during your mix.

4. **Platform Options:** DJ software is highly versatile and available for various platforms, including:

- **Laptop/Desktop:** Most DJs use DJ software on laptop or desktop computers, which offers a powerful and customizable experience.

- **Mobile Devices:** Some DJ software is available as mobile apps, making it convenient for DJs who want to mix on the go using smartphones or tablets.

DJ software has revolutionized DJing by providing DJs with an extensive toolkit to craft unique mixes, experiment with effects, and perform with precision. Whether you're a beginner or a seasoned pro, DJ software is an essential tool that opens up a world of possibilities for creative expression and live performances.

Choosing the Right DJ Software

Choosing the right DJ software is a critical

decision that can significantly impact your DJing experience. Here's a more detailed breakdown of the factors to consider when selecting DJ software:

1. Compatibility:

• **Operating System:** Ensure that the DJ software you choose is compatible with your computer's operating system. Most DJ software works on Windows and macOS, but if you use Linux, compatibility may be more limited.

2. Features:

• **Beatmatching:** Confirm that the software includes beatmatching capabilities, as this is a fundamental DJing skill. Look for features that assist with beatmatching, such as auto-sync.
• **Mixing Tools:** Evaluate the mixing tools available, including crossfaders, EQ controls, and volume adjustments. Some software may offer advanced mixing features like harmonic mixing, which can be valuable for creating harmonious transitions.

• **Effects:** Check if the software provides a variety of effects that align with your creative vision. Different DJ software may offer different effects, so choose one that suits your style.

• **Looping and Cue Points:** If you intend to use loops and cue points extensively in your sets, ensure that the software offers these features and allows for easy setting and triggering.

3. Interface:

• **User-Friendly Design:** The user interface should be intuitive and user-friendly, making it easy for you to navigate and access essential features during your performances.

• **Customization:** Some DJ software allows you to customize the interface, which can be beneficial for creating a workflow that aligns with your preferences.

4. Controller Support:

• **MIDI Controllers:** If you plan to use MIDI controllers (such as DJ controllers or MIDI decks) with the software, ensure that it supports your specific hardware. Compatibility may vary between software options.

- **External Hardware:** Check if the software integrates well with external hardware like sound cards, mixers, or other devices you plan to use in your setup.

5. Cost:

- **Budget:** DJ software comes in a range of price points, from free to premium versions. Determine your budget and choose software that provides the features you need within that budget.
- **Subscription vs. One-Time Purchase:** Some DJ software offers subscription-based models, while others require a one-time purchase. Consider your long-term commitment and budget when making this choice.

6. Trial Version:

- Many DJ software options offer trial versions or free demos. Take advantage of these to test the software's functionality, interface, and compatibility with your hardware before making a commitment.

7. Community and Support:

• Consider the availability of user communities, forums, and customer support for the software. These resources can be valuable for troubleshooting issues, learning new techniques, and seeking assistance from fellow DJs.

Ultimately, the right DJ software choice depends on your specific needs, preferences, and budget. Take your time to research and test different options to find the software that aligns with your DJing style and goals. Your choice of software will play a significant role in shaping your DJing journey and performances.

Digital DJing Techniques

Digital DJing techniques offer a wide array of creative possibilities when using DJ software. Here's a detailed look at these fundamental techniques:

1. Beatmatching:

Beatmatching is the foundation of DJing, ensuring that two tracks play in sync and maintain a consistent tempo. Here's how to beatmatch with DJ software:

- Load two tracks into your DJ software.
- Use the software's waveform display to visually align the beats of both tracks.
- Adjust the tempo (BPM) of one track to match the BPM of the other.
- Use pitch control or sync features to fine-tune the alignment.
- Listen to the tracks together through your headphones and adjust the pitch until they play in perfect sync.

2. Mixing:

Mixing involves transitioning smoothly from one track to another, creating a seamless flow of music. Key mixing techniques include:

- Crossfader: Use the crossfader to gradually fade in one track while fading out the other.
- Volume Levels: Adjust the volume levels of the two tracks to balance their sound during the transition.
- EQ Settings: Use the EQ controls (bass, midrange, treble) to blend the frequencies of the incoming and outgoing tracks.
- Phrase Matching: Transition at appropriate points in the tracks, such as at the end of a phrase or musical section.

3. Effects:

Effects processors in DJ software can enhance your mixes and add creativity. Common effects include:

- **Reverb:** Add a sense of space and depth to your mix.

- **Delay:** Create echoes and rhythmic patterns.
- **Filter:** Manipulate the frequency spectrum for dramatic sweeps.
- **Flanger, Phaser, and Chorus:** Add modulation and movement to your sound.

Experiment with effects to add texture, excitement, and unique elements to your mixes.

4. Looping:

Looping allows you to extend specific sections of a track, build tension, and create repetitive patterns. Here's how to use loops with DJ software:

- Set a loop in and out point on the track.
- Enable the loop, and the selected section will continuously repeat.
- Adjust the loop length and position as needed during your mix.

Looping can be an effective tool for building energy and keeping the dancefloor engaged.

5. Cue Points:

Cue points are markers you set within a track to quickly jump to specific sections during your mix. This technique helps you time your transitions precisely. Here's how to use cue points:

- Set cue points at important sections of the track, such as the intro, breakdown, drop, or outro.
- Trigger cue points using your controller or software interface during your performance.
- Jump to different sections of a track on the fly for creative mixing.

6. Sample Triggering:

Sample triggering involves triggering short audio snippets, such as vocal samples or drum loops, to add layers and complexity to your performance. DJ software often allows you to assign samples to pads or buttons on your controller. Use sample triggering to introduce unique elements into your mix and create memorable moments on the dancefloor.

Mastering these digital DJing techniques, in combination with your creativity and musical intuition, will enable you to craft dynamic and engaging DJ sets that captivate your audience and showcase your unique style. Experimentation and practice are key to refining your skills and developing your DJing prowess.

Using MIDI Controllers

Using MIDI controllers can greatly enhance your control and creativity when DJing with software. Here's a step-by-step guide on how to effectively use MIDI controllers with your DJ software:

1. Connectivity:

• Connect your MIDI controller to your computer using either a USB cable (for USB MIDI controllers) or MIDI cables (for traditional MIDI controllers). Most modern MIDI controllers connect via USB, simplifying the setup.

2. Software Mapping:

- Ensure that your DJ software recognizes your MIDI controller. Most DJ software options support a wide range of MIDI controllers and should automatically detect your device.
- In some cases, you may need to select your MIDI controller from a list of available devices within the software's settings. Refer to your DJ software's user manual for specific instructions on this step.

3. Customization:

- Customize the MIDI controller's mapping to suit your DJing preferences and workflow. This step is crucial for tailoring the controller's functionality to your needs.
- Access your DJ software's MIDI mapping or controller settings section, where you can assign specific functions to the various buttons, knobs, faders, and pads on your controller.
- Map functions such as play/pause, cue points, loop controls, effects parameters, and more to your

controller's elements. You can create custom mappings for different aspects of your DJ performance.

4. Practice:

- Familiarize yourself with your MIDI controller by practicing various DJing techniques using the hardware. This includes practicing beatmatching, mixing, EQ adjustments, and effect manipulation.
- Experiment with your customized mappings to understand how different controls affect your DJ software's functions.

5. Performance:

- Incorporate your MIDI controller into your live DJ performances. During your sets, use the controller to manipulate tracks, trigger samples, and create unique mixes.
- Experiment with different techniques to add a personal touch to your performances. For example, you can use controller pads for sample triggering, knobs for filter sweeps, or faders for precise volume control.

Remember that mastering a MIDI controller takes practice and experimentation. As you become more comfortable with your controller and its mappings, you'll discover new ways to express your creativity and perform unique DJ sets. Additionally, regularly check for firmware updates for your MIDI controller and software to ensure optimal performance and compatibility.

Digital DJing with software and MIDI controllers offers flexibility, creative freedom, and a wide array of tools to take your DJ performances to the next level. Experiment with different software options and MIDI controllers to find the combination that best suits your style and preferences.

Chapter 9: Promoting Yourself as a DJ

Promoting yourself effectively is crucial for building a successful DJ career. In this chapter, we'll explore strategies for creating a DJ brand, networking, building an online presence, and getting gigs. These elements are key to getting your name out there, connecting with your audience, and advancing your DJing career.

Build Experience Gradually

Building experience gradually is an effective approach to developing your skills and confidence as a DJ. Here's a step-by-step guide on how to do it:

1. **Private Practice:** Begin by practicing your DJ skills in a private setting, such as your home or a friend's place. Familiarize yourself

with your equipment, experiment with different mixing techniques, and fine-tune your DJing abilities.

2. **Small Gatherings:** Once you're comfortable with your DJ setup, consider DJing at small gatherings like house parties or get-togethers with friends. These low-pressure events provide an opportunity to perform in a familiar and supportive environment.

3. **Local Events:** Look for opportunities to DJ at local events or venues that cater to emerging DJs. These may include open mic nights, small clubs, or community events. Local gigs allow you to gain experience in a live setting and start building a local fan base.

4. **Residencies:** Consider securing a DJ residency at a local bar, lounge, or club. Residencies provide regular opportunities to DJ and become more accustomed to playing in front of diverse crowds. They also help you establish a consistent presence in your local music scene.

5. **Networking:** Connect with other DJs, event organizers, and promoters in your area.

Networking can lead to more gig opportunities and collaborations. Attend industry events, music festivals, and DJ meetups to expand your network.

6. **Online Platforms:** Use online platforms, such as Mixcloud or SoundCloud, to showcase your DJ sets and gain exposure. Sharing your mixes and tracks online can help you reach a wider audience and attract potential gig offers.

7. **Recorded Sets:** Record your live DJ sets, especially when performing at events. These recordings serve as valuable tools for self-assessment, promotion, and showcasing your skills to potential clients or promoters.

8. **Feedback and Improvement:** Solicit feedback from peers, mentors, and audience members after your performances. Constructive criticism can help you identify areas for improvement and refine your DJing techniques.

9. **Diversify Your Skills:** As you gain experience, explore different DJing styles and genres. Versatility can open up opportunities to DJ at a variety of events and broaden your horizons.

10.   **Promote Yourself:** Create an online presence through a professional website and active social media profiles. Share updates about your gigs, music releases, and DJ journey. Engage with your audience and build a loyal fan base.

11.   **Set Goals:** Establish clear goals for your DJing career. Whether it's landing a residency at a specific venue, performing at a music festival, or releasing your own music, having goals can provide direction and motivation.

12.   **Stay Persistent:** Building a successful DJ career takes time and persistence. There may be setbacks along the way, but maintaining a positive attitude and persevering through challenges is crucial.

13.   **Learn Continuously:** Stay committed to continuous learning. Keep up with industry trends, attend workshops or classes, and invest in improving your skills and knowledge.

14.   **Seek Mentorship:** Consider seeking mentorship from experienced DJs who

can provide guidance, share insights, and help you navigate the DJing industry.

15. **Enjoy the Journey:** Embrace every opportunity to DJ, learn, and grow. Enjoy the journey of becoming a confident and skilled DJ.

By following this gradual progression and consistently honing your skills, you can build the experience and confidence necessary to excel as a DJ and make a significant impact in the music industry.

Creating a DJ Brand

- Defining Your Identity: Develop a clear and unique DJ identity that sets you apart from others. This includes choosing a DJ name, developing a logo, and creating a visual style that represents your brand.
- Brand Consistency: Ensure consistency in your branding across all platforms, from your website and social media profiles to your promotional materials and merchandise.
- Brand Storytelling: Share your DJ journey and personal story with your audience. Connect on a

deeper level by revealing your passion, influences, and motivations.

Networking and Building Connections

- Industry Events: Attend DJ expos, music festivals, club nights, and industry events to meet fellow DJs, promoters, and music industry professionals.
- Local Scene: Get involved in your local music scene by attending and participating in events, collaborating with other artists, and supporting local talent.
- Online Communities: Join online DJ forums, Facebook groups, and platforms like SoundCloud or Mixcloud to connect with DJs and music enthusiasts globally.
- Collaboration: Collaborate with other DJs, producers, and artists on projects, tracks, and events to expand your network and gain exposure.

Social Media and Online Presence

- Social Media Strategy: Develop a social media strategy to effectively engage with your audience on platforms like Facebook, Instagram, Twitter, and TikTok. Share your mixes, behind-the-scenes content, and updates about your DJing journey.

• Website and Blog: Create a professional website that showcases your brand, offers a portfolio of your work, and includes a blog where you can share music-related content and insights.

• Email Marketing: Build an email list to connect directly with your fans. Send newsletters with updates, exclusive mixes, and event announcements.

• Streaming and Podcasts: Consider starting a live streaming series or podcast to regularly engage with your audience and showcase your DJ skills.

Getting Gigs and Booking

• Promo Mixes: Create and share promo mixes that demonstrate your DJing skills and style. These mixes serve as your calling card when approaching venues and promoters.

• Press Kit: Develop a professional press kit that includes your DJ bio, high-quality photos, promo mixes, and contact information. This kit makes it easier for venues and promoters to book you.

- Local Venues: Approach local clubs, bars, and event organizers to express your interest in performing. Attend their events and build relationships with the decision-makers.
- Online Platforms: Use DJ booking platforms like DJ List, Resident Advisor, and GigMasters to list your services and connect with potential clients.
- Networking: Leverage your network and connections in the industry to secure gigs. Recommendations and referrals can open doors to opportunities.
- Self-Promotion: Don't wait for gigs to come to you; actively promote yourself and seek out opportunities. Stay persistent and showcase your dedication to your craft.

By focusing on creating a strong DJ brand, building meaningful connections, maintaining a compelling online presence, and actively seeking gigs, you can elevate your DJ career and increase your chances of success in the competitive world of DJing.

Chapter 10: Legal and Ethical Considerations

In the world of DJing, it's essential to navigate legal and ethical considerations to ensure you operate within the bounds of the law and uphold ethical standards. This chapter delves into key areas of concern:

Copyright and Licensing

Copyright and licensing are fundamental aspects of the music industry, and DJs must understand and adhere to these legal principles. Here's a more detailed look at copyright and licensing considerations for DJs:

Understanding Copyright

• **What Is Copyright:** Copyright is a legal protection granted to creators of original works, including music, to control how their work is used and distributed. It covers various aspects, such as composition (melodies and lyrics) and sound recording (actual audio recordings).

- **Rights of Copyright Holders:** Copyright holders have exclusive rights to reproduce, distribute, perform, and create derivative works based on their music. This means that using copyrighted music without permission can lead to legal issues.
- **Duration of Copyright:** Copyright protection lasts for a specific duration, typically the lifetime of the creator plus 70 years. After this period, the work enters the public domain and can be used without restrictions.

Music Licensing

- **Performance Rights:** When you perform copyrighted music in public, such as at a club or event, you may need a performance license. Venues often handle this licensing, but it's essential to confirm whether they have the necessary agreements in place.
- **Sync Licensing:** If you plan to use music in commercial projects like videos, advertisements, or films, you'll need synchronization (sync) licenses from

both the composition and sound recording copyright holders.

- **Mechanical Licensing:** If you want to create remixes or covers of copyrighted songs, you'll need mechanical licenses to reproduce and distribute those versions.
- **Public Performance Licensing:** Organizations like ASCAP, BMI, and SESAC collect royalties for songwriters and publishers when their music is publicly performed. Venues and event organizers may pay licensing fees to these organizations.

Royalties

- **Performance Royalties:** When your DJ sets are played publicly in venues, clubs, or on the radio, performance royalties are generated. These royalties are collected by performance rights organizations (PROs) and distributed to songwriters and publishers. As a DJ, you typically don't need to handle these royalties directly; venues or PROs take care of them.
- **Digital Royalties:** If you broadcast your DJ sets online, whether through streaming platforms,

podcasts, or live streams, you may be eligible for digital performance royalties. Platforms like SoundExchange collect and distribute these royalties to artists and sound recording copyright holders.

- **Mechanical Royalties:** When you release remixes or sell your DJ mixes, you may be responsible for mechanical royalties. These royalties are paid to songwriters and publishers when their music is reproduced and distributed.

Understanding copyright and licensing is vital to ensure you're using music legally and ethically in your DJing activities. Always obtain the necessary licenses or permissions when required, and be aware of your responsibilities regarding royalties, especially in digital and commercial contexts. Respecting copyright laws not only keeps you on the right side of the law but also supports fellow artists and creators in the music industry.

Respecting Other Artists' Work

Respecting other artists' work is not only an ethical obligation but also a legal necessity for DJs.

Here's a closer look at how to appropriately handle other artists' work in your DJing endeavors:

Crediting Artists

- **Always Give Credit:** When you include another artist's track in your DJ set, whether in a live performance or a recorded mix, always give credit. Mention the track title, artist name, and record label during your set or in any promotional materials associated with your mix.
- **Respect Record Labels:** Record labels play a significant role in music distribution. Acknowledge and respect their contributions by including the label name when crediting a track.
- **Social Media and Playlists:** If you share your DJ sets on social media or music platforms, provide detailed tracklists with proper credits. This not only respects the artists but also helps your audience discover new music.

Remixes and Mashups

- **Obtain Permissions:** If you create remixes or mashups using other artists' tracks, seek the necessary permissions and licenses. Contact the copyright holders of the original tracks, including both the composition (songwriting) and sound recording rights, to ensure you have the legal right to use their material.

- **Use Legal Remixes:** Whenever possible, use officially released and licensed remixes of tracks. These versions have obtained the necessary permissions and clearances, reducing the risk of copyright infringement.

- **Credit Remixers:** If you use official remixes created by other artists, credit them alongside the original track's credits. Acknowledging their work promotes collaboration and respect within the DJ and music community.

Sampling

- **Rights and Clearances:** When using samples from other songs, especially if they are recognizable or substantial, ensure you have the rights to do so. This typically involves obtaining clearance from the copyright holders or using royalty-free samples that are explicitly cleared for use.

- **Royalty-Free and Cleared Samples:** To avoid legal issues, consider using royalty-free and cleared samples in your DJ sets. These samples come with the necessary permissions for use and can be freely incorporated into your mixes.
- **Be Aware of Fair Use:** Be cautious when relying on the "fair use" doctrine in copyright law. Fair use is a complex legal concept, and it's essential to consult with legal experts if you believe your use of copyrighted material falls under fair use.

Respecting the work of other artists not only helps you avoid legal troubles but also fosters a culture of respect and collaboration in the music community. By giving proper credit, obtaining permissions for remixes and mashups, and using samples responsibly, you contribute to the ethical and legal integrity of DJing.

Professionalism and Ethics

Maintaining professionalism and adhering to ethical standards are essential aspects of a successful

DJ career. Here's a closer look at how professionalism and ethics can impact your DJing journey:

Ethical Behavior

- **Respect and Courtesy:** Treat fellow DJs, promoters, venue staff, and other industry professionals with respect and courtesy. Building positive relationships in the music community can lead to valuable opportunities and collaborations.
- **Support Fellow DJs:** Support and uplift fellow DJs rather than engaging in rivalry or negativity. Recognize the talents and contributions of others in the industry.
- **Integrity:** Operate with integrity in all your DJing activities. Honesty, transparency, and fairness should be at the core of your interactions with others.

Promotion

- **Honesty in Marketing:** When promoting your DJ services, be honest and transparent. Avoid exaggerations or false claims about your skills, achievements, or experience. Authenticity resonates with your audience and builds trust.

- **Accurate Representation:** Ensure that your promotional materials, such as press kits, bios, and social media profiles, accurately represent your abilities and style as a DJ.

- **Respect Copyright:** In your promotional content, respect copyright laws by obtaining the necessary permissions for music usage and properly crediting artists and labels.

Punctuality

- **Arrival and Commitment:** Punctuality is a hallmark of professionalism. Arrive on time for your gigs and fulfill your commitments as agreed upon with venues, clients, and collaborators.

- **Communication:** If unforeseen circumstances affect your ability to be punctual, communicate promptly with relevant parties to provide notice and work toward a solution.

- **Reliability:** Consistently demonstrating punctuality and reliability enhances your reputation and encourages repeat bookings and positive word-of-mouth referrals.

Maintaining professionalism and adhering to ethical principles not only reflect positively on your DJ career but also contribute to a healthy and vibrant music community. Building a reputation as a reliable, respectful, and ethical DJ can lead to long-term success and meaningful connections in the industry.

Contracts and Agreements

Contracts and agreements are vital tools for protecting your interests, setting clear expectations, and ensuring smooth business interactions in your DJing career. Here's a deeper look at the importance of contracts and key elements to include:

Written Agreements

- **Clear Terms:** A written agreement provides clarity on the terms and conditions of your DJ gig or collaboration. It outlines what is expected of both parties and prevents misunderstandings.

- **Legal Protection:** A signed contract is a legally binding document that offers protection to both you and your client or collaborator. It establishes the framework for your working relationship.

- **Professionalism:** Using contracts demonstrates professionalism and seriousness in your DJ career. It instills confidence in clients and collaborators.

- **Template Use:** Consider using template contracts tailored to your specific needs. Templates can help streamline the contract creation process while ensuring essential terms are covered.

Payment Terms

- **Fees and Expenses:** Clearly specify your fees, including any additional expenses such as travel, accommodation, or equipment rental, in the contract.

- **Payment Schedule:** Define the payment schedule, including due dates and the method of payment. This ensures that you receive compensation according to the agreed-upon terms.
- **Deposits:** Consider including a deposit clause. Deposits are often paid in advance to secure your services and mitigate the risk of cancellations.
- **Late Payment:** Address late payment penalties or interest charges if payments are not made on time.

Cancellation Policies:

- **Cancellation Terms:** Detail the terms surrounding cancellations, including notice periods and penalties. Specify what happens if either party decides to cancel the engagement.
- **Force Majeure:** Include a force majeure clause to address unforeseen circumstances, such as natural disasters or emergencies, that may affect the event or collaboration.
- **Rescheduling:** Outline the process for rescheduling in case of cancellations or unforeseen

events. Determine who bears the responsibility for rescheduling and any associated costs.

• **Refunds:** Clarify the refund policy in case of cancellations, ensuring both parties understand their rights and obligations.

Contracts and agreements play a crucial role in maintaining professionalism, protecting your interests, and avoiding disputes in your DJing career. While standard templates can be a helpful starting point, it's advisable to consult with legal professionals or seek industry-specific guidance when drafting or signing contracts, especially for significant gigs or collaborations. Clear and comprehensive agreements help you navigate the complexities of the DJing business with confidence.

Navigating the legal and ethical aspects of DJing is essential for maintaining your professional reputation and avoiding legal troubles. Staying informed about copyright laws, obtaining the necessary licenses, respecting other artists' work, and adhering to ethical standards will help you build a sustainable and reputable DJ career. Additionally, having clear contracts and agreements in place ensures that all parties involved understand their obligations and rights, minimizing potential disputes.

Chapter 11: Advanced DJing Skills

Advanced DJing skills can set you apart and take your performances to the next level. Here's a closer look at some of these skills:

Live remixing and mashups are advanced DJing techniques that add creativity and uniqueness to your performances. Here's a more detailed look at these skills:

Live Remixing

Live remixing is the art of transforming tracks on the spot during your DJ sets. It involves real-time manipulation of audio elements like effects, loops, samples, and more. Here's how to excel in live remixing:

- **Controller Setup:** To perform live remixing, you'll need a DJ controller or software with performance pads, effects controls, and sample triggering capabilities. Familiarize yourself with your controller's layout.

- **Effects Integration:** Integrate effects processors into your DJ setup. Experiment with effects like filter sweeps, delays, and reverbs to add texture and dynamics to your mixes.

- **Looping and Sampling:** Use loops and samples creatively to enhance tracks. Looping a catchy section or dropping unexpected samples can surprise and delight your audience.

- **Timing and Practice:** Timing is crucial in live remixing. Practice your timing and transitions to ensure that your remixes seamlessly integrate with the tracks you're playing.

- **Experimentation:** Don't be afraid to experiment with different effects, samples, and remixing techniques. The more you explore, the more unique and personalized your live remixes will become.

Mashups

Mashups involve blending elements from multiple tracks to create a new, cohesive composition. Here are steps to create compelling mashups:

- **Selecting Tracks:** Choose tracks that have compatible tempos, keys, and musical elements. Experiment with different combinations to find those that work well together.
- **Acquiring Stems:** If possible, obtain the stems (individual tracks or elements) of the songs you want to mash up. Stems provide greater control and flexibility in your mashup.
- **Sync and Timing:** Ensure that the tracks are properly synced. Use DJ software or controllers to beatmatch and align the tracks' timing.
- **Layering:** Blend the vocals or instrumental sections of one track with the instrumental or vocals of another. Experiment with different arrangements and transitions to create a seamless mashup.
- **Editing and Post-Production:** Use audio editing software to fine-tune your mashup. This may involve adjusting levels, EQ, and adding effects for a polished result.
- **Practice:** Practice your mashups extensively to ensure flawless execution during your sets. A well-

executed mashup can be a highlight of your performance.

Live remixing and mashups allow you to add a personal touch to your DJ sets, creating memorable moments that resonate with your audience. These skills require both technical proficiency and creative experimentation. With dedication and practice, you can become a skilled live remixer and mashup artist, setting your DJing apart from the rest.

Harmonic Mixing

Harmonic mixing is an advanced DJing technique that involves mixing tracks that are harmonically compatible in terms of their musical keys. By matching the keys of songs, DJs can create harmonious transitions and enhance the musicality of their sets. Here's a deeper dive into harmonic mixing and how to incorporate it into your DJ performances:

Understanding Harmonic Mixing

- **Musical Keys:** In music theory, each song is typically associated with a specific musical key. The key of a song determines its tonal center and the set of notes and chords that work well together within that key.

- **Harmonic Compatibility:** Harmonic mixing involves selecting tracks that share harmonically compatible keys. This means choosing songs whose keys are closely related or compatible, creating a smoother and more pleasing transition between tracks.

- **Camelot Wheel:** Many DJs use the Camelot Wheel or a similar system to easily identify harmonically compatible keys. This system assigns a unique code to each key, making it easier to find compatible tracks quickly.

Tips for Harmonic Mixing

1. **Learn Basic Music Theory:** Familiarize yourself with basic music theory concepts, including scales, keys, and chord progressions. Understanding these fundamentals will help you identify compatible keys.

2. **Use Key Detection Software:** Utilize key detection software or features available in DJ software to analyze the keys of your music library. This can save you time when searching for compatible tracks.

3. **Study the Camelot Wheel:** Learn how to use the Camelot Wheel or a similar key compatibility system. This visual aid simplifies the process of finding harmonically compatible tracks.

4. **Practice with Compatible Tracks:** Start by mixing tracks that are harmonically compatible. This will help you get a feel for how well the technique works and build your confidence.

5. **Plan Your Set:** Plan the harmonic progression of your DJ set. Begin with tracks in one key and gradually transition to tracks in related keys. This creates a seamless and pleasing journey for the audience.

6. **Experiment with Transitions:** Explore different mixing techniques that work well with harmonic mixing, such as blending, EQing, and using effects. Experiment with creative ways to enhance the transitions between tracks.

7. **Listen Actively:** Pay close attention to how harmonically mixed tracks complement each other. Train your ears to detect when a transition is harmonically pleasing.

8. **Record and Analyze Sets:** Record your DJ sets and analyze them to assess your harmonic mixing skills. Identify areas where you can improve your transitions and track selection.

9. **Balance Energy:** While harmonic mixing is important for musicality, remember to balance it with track energy and crowd engagement. Sometimes, a slight key clash can create tension and excitement in the mix.

10. **Trust Your Ears:** While harmonic mixing guidelines can be helpful, ultimately, trust your ears and musical intuition. Sometimes, a harmonic "rule" can be bent or broken for creative effect.

Harmonic mixing is a technique that adds a layer of musical sophistication to your DJ sets. It enhances the flow and emotional impact of your mixes and can make your performances more memorable and enjoyable for your audience.

Harmonic mixing requires practice and a good understanding of music theory, particularly key relationships. While it's not necessary to be a music theory expert, having a basic grasp of keys and using key detection software can significantly enhance your DJing skills and the overall listening experience. It's can set your DJ sets apart and make them more enjoyable and memorable.

DVS (Digital Vinyl Systems)

Digital Vinyl Systems (DVS) offer a unique and hybrid DJing experience by combining the traditional feel of vinyl with the flexibility of digital DJing. Here's a closer look at DVS:

DVS Basics

DVS technology bridges the gap between analog vinyl and digital audio files. It allows DJs to control and manipulate digital music using conventional vinyl records or CDJs, giving them the tactile and responsive feel of vinyl while accessing the extensive capabilities of digital DJ software.

Setup

To set up a DVS system, you'll need the following components:

1. **DVS-Compatible Mixer:** You'll need a DJ mixer that supports DVS technology. These mixers have built-in sound cards and inputs for connecting turntables or CDJs.

2. **Timecode Vinyl Records or Control CDs:** Timecode vinyl records (for turntables) or control CDs (for CDJs) are special vinyl or CDs encoded with a time-stamped signal that communicates with the DVS software. This signal allows the software to track the movement and position of the vinyl or CD.

3. **DJ Software:** Choose DJ software that is compatible with DVS. Popular options include Serato DJ, Traktor Scratch, and Virtual DJ. Install the software on your computer and configure it to work with your DVS setup.

4. **Turntables or CDJs:** You'll need traditional turntables (with appropriate DVS-compatible cartridges) or CDJs to play the timecode vinyl records

or control CDs. These will serve as your primary control surface.

5. **Audio Interface:** Some DVS setups may require an external audio interface to route audio between your computer and mixer.

Precise Control

DVS systems provide DJs with precise control over their digital music library. Here's how it works:

- When you play a timecode vinyl record or control CD on a turntable or CDJ, the DVS software interprets the time-stamped signal and translates it into digital audio.

- This digital audio is then processed by the DJ software, allowing you to scratch, cue, and mix digital tracks using the vinyl or CD as your control surface.

- DJs can use traditional vinyl techniques like scratching, backspins, and pitch control while having access to their entire digital music collection.

- DVS setups are particularly favored by turntablists and vinyl enthusiasts who appreciate the tactile experience of vinyl while taking advantage of the convenience and versatility of digital DJing.

DVS technology has revolutionized the DJ industry by preserving the art of vinyl manipulation while seamlessly integrating digital music libraries. It's a versatile and powerful tool that offers DJs the best of both worlds.

DJing with Effects

DJing with effects is a creative technique that allows DJs to add depth, texture, and unique sonic elements to their mixes. Here's a more detailed explanation of this skill:

Effects Processors

DJing with effects involves using audio effects processors to manipulate the sound of your tracks. These processors can be external hardware units or software-based effects within your DJ software. Common effects used in DJing include:

1. **Reverb:** Adds a sense of space and depth to your mix, creating the impression of sound in a larger environment.

2. **Delay:** Repeats the audio signal, creating echoes or echoes with varying delay times. It can add a sense of rhythm and atmosphere to your mix.

3. **Phaser:** Modifies the phase of the audio signal to create a sweeping, swirling effect. It's often used to add a psychedelic or futuristic texture to the sound.

4. **Flanger:** Similar to a phaser but with a different modulation pattern, flanger effects create a distinctive whooshing or jet plane-like sound.

5. **Filter:** Alters the frequency response of the audio, allowing you to emphasize or suppress specific frequencies. Filters can be used for dramatic build-ups and drops.

6. **Bitcrusher:** Adds distortion and quantization noise to create a lo-fi, retro sound.

Effect Routing

Understanding the routing and manipulation of effects in real-time is crucial for effective DJing with effects. Here's how you can use them effectively:

1. **Effect Placement:** Decide where in the audio signal chain you want to apply effects. Common options include sending effects to individual channels, using an auxiliary send/return system, or applying effects to the master output for global processing.

2. **Effect Parameters:** Familiarize yourself with the parameters of each effect, including wet/dry mix, feedback, decay, modulation depth, and more. These parameters allow you to shape the effect to your liking.

3. **Automation:** Many DJ software and hardware controllers allow you to automate effect parameters over time. This can create dynamic and evolving soundscapes during your sets.

Subtle Application

While effects can be powerful tools for creativity, it's essential to use them judiciously. Here are some tips for subtle and effective use of effects:

- Less Is More: Avoid overusing effects, as too much processing can clutter your mix and overwhelm the audience.
- Listen and React: Pay close attention to the tracks you're mixing and the audience's reaction. Apply effects when they enhance the moment or create a specific mood.
- Practice: Experiment with different effects and practice using them in your sets to develop your understanding of their subtleties.
- Blend Effectively: Use the wet/dry mix control to blend the affected signal with the dry signal. This allows you to add just the right amount of effect.
- Know Your Effects: Understand the characteristics and sonic impact of each effect you use. This knowledge will help you make informed decisions when applying effects.

DJing with effects is a skill that can set you apart as a creative DJ. When used thoughtfully and with a deep understanding of your tools, effects can elevate your mixes, create memorable moments, and captivate your audience.

Mastering these advanced DJing skills takes

practice, experimentation, and a deep understanding of music theory, technology, and performance techniques. As you develop these skills, you'll have the tools to create captivating and innovative DJ sets that leave a lasting impression on your audience.

Chapter 12: The Future of DJing

The future of DJing is shaped by various factors, including technological advancements, changes in music consumption, and evolving audience preferences. Here's a glimpse into the future of DJing:

Trends in DJ Technology

Advanced Software and Hardware Integration: The continued integration of software and hardware offers DJs more seamless and creative control over their performances. Future DJ setups may involve even tighter integration between controllers, mixers, and software, enabling DJs to have more intuitive and expressive control over their music. This could lead to the development of innovative DJ equipment that responds to gestures, touch, and other forms of expressive input.

AI and Machine Learning: The incorporation of AI and machine learning into DJ software holds significant potential. AI can assist DJs in various ways, such as automatically beatmatching tracks, suggesting compatible songs based on a chosen track, and even dynamically adjusting the mix to match the energy of the crowd. This can free up DJs to focus on creativity and performance while AI handles some of the technical aspects.

Gesture Control: Gesture-based control interfaces can add a new layer of interactivity and creativity to DJ performances. DJs may use hand movements, gestures, or motion-sensing technology to manipulate sound, effects, and visuals in real-time. This can lead to more engaging and visually captivating live shows, as well as open up opportunities for audience participation.

VR and AR Integration: VR and AR have the potential to revolutionize the live DJ experience. DJs could perform in virtual environments that are limited only by their imagination, creating immersive and visually stunning shows. AR could enhance the DJ's view of the audience, providing real-time feedback on crowd reactions and preferences, allowing for more responsive and dynamic sets.

Blockchain and Music Rights: The use of blockchain technology to manage music rights and royalties could bring transparency and fairness to the music industry. Smart contracts on blockchain networks can automate royalty payments to artists, ensuring that they are compensated fairly when their music is played by DJs in various contexts. This can have a profound impact on how artists and DJs collaborate and distribute their music.

As these trends continue to develop, DJs will need to adapt and embrace new technologies to stay at the forefront of the industry. Embracing these innovations can lead to more creative and immersive DJ performances while ensuring fair compensation for artists and creators. The future of DJing holds exciting possibilities for both DJs and music enthusiasts.

The Impact of Streaming Services

The impact of streaming services on DJing is profound and continues to shape how DJs access, manage, and perform with music. Let's delve deeper into these aspects:

Access to Vast Music Libraries: Streaming services have democratized access to music, providing DJs with an extensive and ever-growing catalog of tracks from various genres and eras. This trend allows DJs to explore a wider range of music, experiment with new genres, and cater to diverse audiences. It also reduces the need for DJs to purchase individual tracks, which can be cost-effective in the long run.

Real-Time Track Updates: Streaming platforms have the advantage of real-time updates to track metadata, including BPM, key, and artist information.

This feature can significantly streamline the DJ's workflow, making it easier to organize and prepare sets. DJs can access up-to-date information about their music library, ensuring accurate track selection and mixing.

Collaboration Opportunities: Streaming services can potentially facilitate real-time collaboration among DJs and producers. DJs can share playlists and tracks with one another, making it easier to collaborate on live remixes and mashups during performances. This opens up exciting possibilities for dynamic and spontaneous collaborations between artists and DJs.

However, it's essential for DJs to consider some key aspects:

1. **Internet Connectivity:** Reliance on streaming services requires a stable internet connection, which may not always be available in certain venues or during outdoor events. DJs should have contingency plans, such as downloading essential tracks for offline use.

2. **Sound Quality:** While streaming services offer convenience, DJs may need to consider the sound quality of the tracks they access. Some may prefer to obtain high-quality files for critical performances, ensuring the best possible audio experience.

3. **Legal and Licensing Considerations:** DJs should be aware of the licensing and copyright implications of using streamed tracks in live performances. Some venues or events may require specific licensing agreements for streaming use, and DJs should ensure they are compliant with legal requirements.

4. **Backup Plans:** To mitigate potential technical issues or interruptions, DJs should always have backup tracks and equipment ready. Streaming should complement their music library, not be the sole source of music during performances.

In summary, streaming services have revolutionized the DJing landscape by providing DJs with unparalleled access to music. DJs should embrace these opportunities while also being mindful of potential challenges and considerations to ensure smooth and legal use of streamed music in their performances.

Advice from Top DJs

The advice from top DJs is not only valuable but also timeless. These principles can guide both aspiring and established DJs on their journey to becoming skilled and respected artists. Let's explore each of these pieces of wisdom in more detail:

1. Practice and Persistence: DJing, like any craft, requires dedication and consistent practice. It's through practice that you refine your skills, develop muscle memory, and gain confidence in your abilities. Regular practice helps you become more comfortable with your equipment, music selection, and the art of mixing. The more you practice, the more effortless your performances will become.

2. Trust Your Ears: Developing a keen ear for music is fundamental for DJs. It involves honing your ability to recognize beat patterns, key harmonies, and the nuances of tracks. Trusting your ears means relying on your intuition and musical instincts when selecting and mixing tracks. This skill grows with experience and attentive listening.

3. Be Authentic: Your authenticity as a DJ is your unique selling point. It's what sets you apart from other DJs and creates a distinct identity. Discover your musical preferences, style, and the genres that resonate with you the most. Embrace your individuality, and let it shine through in your sets. Authenticity not only attracts fans but also fuels your passion for DJing.

4. Stay Humble: The DJing landscape is continually evolving, with new technologies, genres, and trends emerging. No matter your level of success, it's essential to remain humble and open to learning. There's always more to explore, whether it's mastering new techniques, discovering underground artists, or adapting to changing audience preferences. Humility keeps you curious and adaptable.

5. Connect with Your Audience: Successful DJing isn't just about playing music; it's about creating memorable experiences for your audience. Learning to read the crowd, understand their energy, and adjust your set accordingly is a valuable skill. Building a connection with your audience through music can lead to loyal fans and unforgettable performances.

6. Take Risks: DJing is an art form that thrives on creativity and innovation. Don't be afraid to step outside your comfort zone and experiment with new tracks, mixing techniques, or effects. Taking risks can lead to exciting and unexpected results, sparking creativity and making your sets stand out.

Incorporating these principles into your DJing journey can help you not only become a skilled DJ but also a respected and memorable one. Remember that DJing is both a craft and an art, and it's the combination of technical skill and creative expression that makes it such a captivating and rewarding pursuit.

As you conclude this journey into the world of DJing, it's essential to take a moment to reflect on your own path and the knowledge and skills you've gained along the way. Whether you're an aspiring DJ taking your first steps or an experienced DJ seeking to refine your craft, the journey of DJing is a dynamic and rewarding one.

Consider the following points as you reflect on your DJ journey:

1. **Progress and Growth:** Take stock of how far you've come and the progress you've made as a DJ. Celebrate your achievements, whether they involve mastering a particular technique, performing at a memorable event, or simply expanding your music collection.

2. **Challenges and Learning:** Acknowledge the challenges you've faced and the lessons you've learned from them. DJing, like any creative pursuit, has its share of obstacles, but each challenge presents an opportunity for growth and improvement.

3. **Musical Identity:** Reflect on your musical identity and the unique style you've developed as a DJ. What sets you apart from others in the DJing community? Embrace your individuality and continue to explore and refine your style.

4. **Audience Connection:** Think about the connections you've established with your audience. The ability to engage and move a crowd is a testament to your skill as a DJ. Building and nurturing these connections can lead to a rewarding and enduring career.

5. **Future Aspirations:** Consider your future aspirations as a DJ. What do you hope to achieve in your DJing career? Whether it's performing on larger stages, producing original tracks, or mentoring the next generation of DJs, setting clear goals can help guide your journey.

The Endless Possibilities of DJing

DJing is an art form with limitless possibilities. It's a journey of constant discovery, where creativity knows no bounds. As you continue on your DJing path, remember that the possibilities are endless:

- **Musical Exploration:** Dive deeper into the world of music, exploring new genres, eras, and cultures. The more diverse your musical palette, the richer your DJ sets can become.

- **Technical Innovation:** Stay abreast of the latest DJ technologies and innovations. As DJ gear evolves, you'll have the opportunity to experiment with cutting-edge tools and techniques.

- **Collaboration:** Collaborate with other artists, whether they're fellow DJs, producers, or live performers. Collaborations can lead to exciting and unique projects that push the boundaries of your creativity.

- **Performance Venues:** DJing can take you to a wide range of venues, from intimate clubs to massive festivals, and even virtual spaces. Each setting presents its own challenges and opportunities for artistic expression.

- **Musical Production:** If you haven't already explored music production, consider it as a way to create your own original tracks. Producing your music can be a natural extension of your DJing journey.

- **Mentoring and Sharing:** Share your knowledge and experience with others, whether through mentoring aspiring DJs or contributing to the DJing community. Passing on your wisdom can be a fulfilling way to give back.

In the world of DJing, your journey is ongoing, and the possibilities are boundless. Embrace the art, the craft, and the culture of DJing with passion and curiosity, and you'll continue to find inspiration and growth at every turn. Your DJ journey is a voyage of discovery and self-expression, and it's a journey worth savoring every step of the way.

Appendices

In addition to the comprehensive content covered in the main chapters of this book, we've included a set of appendices to further enhance your DJing knowledge and resources. These appendices are designed to be valuable references and tools as you continue your journey in the world of DJing.

Glossary of DJ Terminology

A

Acoustics: The science of sound, including its production, transmission, and effects. Understanding acoustics is important for setting up sound systems in venues.

Analog: Refers to traditional, non-digital audio equipment or signals. Analog turntables, mixers, and vinyl records are examples.

B

Backspin: A DJ technique where a track is briefly reversed (spun backward) and then quickly released to create a distinctive sound effect.

Beatmatching: The process of aligning the beats (rhythmic pulses) of two tracks so they play in sync, a fundamental DJ skill.

Booth Monitor: A speaker or monitor placed in the DJ booth to allow the DJ to hear the mix independently of the main PA system.

Break: A short section of a track, often characterized by a drum solo or instrumental passage. DJs may use breaks for mixing or adding effects.

C

Cue: A point in a track where a DJ sets a marker to start playback. Cue points help DJs quickly jump to specific parts of a track.

Cue Mix: The ability to adjust the headphone mix between the live audio from the main mix and the cue audio from the headphones, allowing DJs to preview upcoming tracks.

D

Deck: A term used to refer to a turntable or a DJ controller that represents one side or source of audio. DJs typically have two decks for mixing.

Digital Vinyl System (DVS): A system that allows DJs to control digital music using traditional vinyl records or control CDs, often with the help of timecode technology.

Drop: The moment in a track where a significant and often energetic element, such as a bassline or a beat, kicks in. It's a key point for building energy on the dancefloor.

E

Effects: Audio processing tools that DJs use to modify the sound of tracks in real-time. Common effects include reverb, delay, and phaser.

Equalization (EQ): The process of adjusting the balance of frequencies (bass, midrange, treble) in a track to achieve a desired sound.

F

Fader: A sliding control on a mixer used to adjust the volume of an audio channel. Crossfaders are commonly used for smooth transitions between tracks.

Feedback: Unwanted, high-pitched noise produced when a microphone picks up the sound of a speaker and re-amplifies it. It's essential to avoid feedback in live DJ setups.

Filter: An effect used to attenuate or boost specific frequency ranges in a track, creating a filtering or sweeping sound.

H

Headphones: Audio headphones are essential for cueing and monitoring tracks before they are mixed into the main output.

J

Jog Wheel: A rotating, touch-sensitive wheel on DJ controllers and CDJs used for manipulating the playback position of a track, including scratching.

K

Key: The musical key or pitch of a track. Harmonic mixing involves mixing tracks that share the same or compatible keys.

L

Loop: A section of a track that is repeated seamlessly. Looping is used for extending sections of songs or creating tension and energy.

M

MIDI (Musical Instrument Digital Interface): A protocol that allows electronic musical instruments, including DJ controllers, to communicate with computers and other MIDI devices.

Mixer: The central component of a DJ setup that allows DJs to blend and control multiple audio sources. It includes channels, EQs, and faders.

P

Pitch Control: A feature that allows DJs to adjust the speed (pitch) of a track to match the tempo of another track, essential for beatmatching.

Punch-In/Out: A technique where a DJ momentarily activates a track, sound, or effect during a mix for dramatic impact.

R

Reverb: An effect that simulates the sound reflection and diffusion in physical spaces, adding depth and space to the audio.

S

Scratching: A turntablism technique where DJs manipulate the sound of a track by moving a vinyl record back and forth against a stylus.

Serato: A popular brand of digital DJ software and hardware, often used with DVS systems.

Sync: A feature in DJ software that automatically synchronizes the beats of two tracks, making beatmatching easier.

T

Timecode: A control signal used in DVS systems, usually encoded on vinyl records or control CDs, to track the position and speed of the playback.

Traktor: A popular brand of DJ software and hardware developed by Native Instruments.

V

Vinyl: Traditional records made of vinyl with grooves that contain audio information. Vinyl records are still used by many DJs, especially in turntablism.

Recommended Reading and Resources

1. "How to DJ Right: The Art and Science of Playing Records" by Frank Broughton and Bill Brewster - A comprehensive guide covering the history, techniques, and philosophy of DJing.
2. "Last Night a DJ Saved My Life: The History of the Disc Jockey" by Bill Brewster and Frank

Broughton - An engaging exploration of DJ culture and its impact on music.

3. "The DJ Sales and Marketing Handbook: How to Achieve Success, Grow Your Business, and Get Paid to Party!" by Stacy Zemon - A resource for aspiring DJ entrepreneurs looking to market and grow their DJ business.

4. "DJing for Dummies" by John Steventon - A beginner-friendly guide covering the essentials of DJing, equipment, and techniques.

5. "The Record Players: DJ Revolutionaries" by Bill Brewster and Frank Broughton - An in-depth look at the lives and stories of pioneering DJs who shaped the DJ culture.

Websites and Forums

1. **Digital DJ Tips** - Offers articles, courses, and a community forum for DJs of all levels.

2. **DJ TechTools** - Provides reviews, tutorials, and resources related to DJ equipment and technology.

3. **Serato** - The official website of Serato DJ software, offering tutorials and support.

4. **Pioneer DJ** - Pioneer's official website features product information and resources for DJ equipment.

5. **DJforum** - An active online community where DJs share knowledge and discuss various DJing topics.

Online Courses:

1. **Point Blank Music School** - Offers online DJ courses covering various aspects of DJing and music production.

2. **Berklee Online** - Provides courses in DJing, music production, and related topics for those looking to earn a degree.

3. **DJ Courses Online** - Offers a variety of online DJ courses for beginners and advanced DJs.

4. **Crossfader** - Provides online DJ courses and tutorials, including beginner to advanced levels.

5. **Skillshare** - Offers a range of DJing courses and tutorials on various aspects of music and audio production.

Explore these resources to deepen your knowledge, develop your skills, and stay up-to-date with the latest trends and techniques in the world of DJing. Whether you're a beginner or an experienced DJ, there's always more to learn and discover.

DJ Equipment Buying Guide

Investing in the right DJ equipment is crucial for your journey into the world of DJing. The choices you make will significantly impact your performance and the quality of your sets. Here's a buying guide to help you make informed decisions:

1. Understand Your DJing Style

Before purchasing equipment, consider the type of DJing you want to pursue. Are you interested in turntablism, club DJing, mobile DJing, or something else? Your style will dictate the gear you need.

2. DJ Software and Controllers

a. DJ Software: Decide on the DJ software you want to use. Popular choices include Serato DJ, Traktor Pro, Rekordbox, and Virtual DJ. Some software is free, while others come with a price tag. Make sure it's compatible with your operating system (Windows, macOS, etc.).

b. Controllers: Many DJs prefer to use DJ controllers, which offer a tactile experience for software-based DJing. Look for controllers that match your software and offer the features you need. Consider factors like the number of channels, jog wheel size, and built-in pads.

3. Turntables and CDJs

a. Turntables: If you're interested in vinyl DJing, invest in a pair of high-quality turntables. Look for features like direct drive (for stability), adjustable pitch control, and replaceable cartridges.

b. CDJs: CDJs are essential for club DJs. Choose models that are club-standard and include features like pitch control, cue points, and looping functions.

4. Mixers

The mixer is the heart of your DJ setup. Consider:

a. Channels: Decide how many channels you need. Two channels are sufficient for basic mixing, but four channels allow for more advanced mixing techniques.

b. Effects: Some mixers come with built-in effects processors. If you plan to use effects extensively, consider a mixer with these capabilities.

c. Size and Portability: Think about whether you need a compact mixer for portability or a larger one with more features.

5. Headphones

Choose closed-back headphones with good sound isolation. Look for comfort and durability, as you'll wear them for extended periods during gigs.

6. Speakers (PA Systems)

a. Configuration: Decide between two-way and three-way speaker systems. Two-way speakers are suitable for most DJ setups, while three-way systems offer enhanced audio fidelity.

b. Power Rating: Consider the power rating (wattage) of your speakers, ensuring they can handle the venues where you'll perform.

c. Placement: Think about speaker placement for optimal sound coverage. Consider whether you need additional subwoofers for bass reinforcement.

7. Choosing the Right Location

When setting up your DJ gear, consider factors like space, electrical outlets, and acoustics in the venue.

8. Assembling Your DJ Setup

Follow a step-by-step guide for setting up your equipment, from positioning turntables or controllers to connecting them to the mixer and speakers. Manage your cables for an organized and safe setup.

9. Powering On and Off

Learn to power on and off your DJ gear safely to avoid damage and ensure a smooth start to your sessions.

10. Types of Audio Cables

Understand common audio cables used in DJ setups, including RCA, XLR, and 1/4-inch TRS cables. Learn their purpose and usage.

11. Cable Connections

Know how to correctly connect and disconnect audio cables to your equipment, ensuring optimal audio quality and preventing damage. Learn troubleshooting tips for common cable-related issues.

With this buying guide, you'll make informed decisions when investing in DJ equipment, whether you're a beginner or upgrading your existing setup. Your choice of gear will shape your DJing experience, so take your time and choose wisely.

Sample Contracts and Agreements

As a DJ, it's essential to have clear agreements and contracts in place when booking gigs and events. These templates can serve as a starting point for negotiations with event organizers, venues, and clients. Make sure to tailor them to your specific needs and consult with legal counsel if necessary.

1. DJ Performance Agreement

[DJ Name] ("DJ") agrees to provide DJ services at [Event Name] ("Event") on [Event Date] at [Event Location].

Terms and Conditions:

1. **Performance Fee:** The client agrees to pay the DJ a performance fee of [Agreed Fee], which includes [list any inclusions, e.g., equipment setup, lighting, sound system].

2. **Payment:** A non-refundable deposit of [Deposit Amount] is due upon the signing of this agreement. The remaining balance is due in full on or before [Event Date].

3. **Cancellation:** In the event of cancellation by the client, the deposit is non-refundable. Cancellation by the DJ will result in a full refund of the deposit.

4. **Equipment and Setup:** The DJ will provide all necessary equipment for the performance,

including [list equipment]. The client agrees to provide adequate space and power outlets.

5. **Performance Hours:** The DJ will perform from [Start Time] to [End Time]. Overtime may be requested and will be charged at [Overtime Rate] per hour.

6. **Music Selection:** The client may request specific songs or genres to be included in the DJ's performance. However, the DJ retains the right to make adjustments as needed to maintain the flow of the event.

7. **Liability:** The DJ is not responsible for any damage to the venue or its property caused by event attendees.

8. **Insurance:** The DJ will carry liability insurance for the event.

9. **Force Majeure:** In the event of unforeseen circumstances, such as natural disasters or emergencies, either party may terminate this agreement without penalty.

10. **Legal Compliance:** The DJ agrees to comply with all copyright and licensing laws, and the client ensures all necessary licenses for the performance.

Signatures:

[DJ Name] [Client Name]

[Date] [Date]

[DJ Signature] [Client Signature]

2. Venue Rental Agreement

[Venue Name] ("Venue") agrees to provide a space for [DJ Name] ("DJ") to perform on [Event Date] at [Event Location].

Terms and Conditions:

1. **Venue Rental Fee:** The DJ agrees to pay the Venue a rental fee of [Rental Fee].

2. **Payment:** The rental fee is due in full on or before [Event Date].

3. **Equipment and Setup:** The Venue will provide the following equipment and facilities for the event: [List equipment and facilities provided].

4. **Liability:** The DJ is responsible for any damage to the Venue or its property caused by the DJ or event attendees.

5. **Insurance:** The DJ will carry liability insurance for the event.

6. **Force Majeure:** In the event of unforeseen circumstances, such as natural disasters or emergencies, either party may terminate this agreement without penalty.

7. **Legal Compliance:** The DJ agrees to comply with all copyright and licensing laws, and the Venue ensures all necessary licenses for the performance.

Signatures:

[Venue Name] [DJ Name]

[Date] [Date]

[Venue Signature] [DJ Signature]

These sample contracts and agreements provide a starting point for negotiations and can help protect your interests when booking DJ gigs and events. Always consult with legal counsel to ensure that your agreements comply with local laws and regulations.

DJing Exercises and Practice Routines

Becoming a skilled DJ requires consistent practice and honing of your skills. These exercises and routines cover various aspects of DJing, from fundamental techniques to advanced mixing and performance skills. Whether you're a beginner looking to build a strong foundation or an experienced DJ looking to refine your craft, regular practice is key to success.

Exercise 1: Beatmatching Basics

Objective: Practice beatmatching by manually aligning the beats of two tracks.

1. Select two tracks with matching BPM (e.g., house or techno tracks around 120 BPM).

2. Load one track onto each deck of your DJ setup.

3. Start one track playing on Deck A.

4. Start the second track playing on Deck B.

5. Listen carefully and use pitch control to adjust the speed of Deck B until the beats of both tracks align perfectly. Pay attention to the phasing sound, which indicates whether the beats are aligned or not.

6. Once the beats are perfectly matched, practice crossfading between the two tracks.

7. Experiment with pitch bending and nudging to keep the beats in sync during the mix.

8. Repeat this exercise with different tracks and BPMs to improve your beatmatching skills.

Exercise 2: Phrasing and Transitions

Objective: Practice transitioning between tracks at the right phrase to create seamless mixes.

1. Choose two tracks that have distinct phrases, such as a breakdown or drop.

2. Load one track onto each deck.

3. Listen to both tracks and identify the phrases (e.g., 16-bar or 32-bar phrases).

4. Start playing the first track and let it play until it reaches a phrase change.

5. At the right moment, start the second track on the other deck so that it aligns with the phrase change of the first track.

6. Use EQ, filters, and volume faders to smoothly transition between the tracks.

7. Practice this exercise with different tracks and pay attention to phrasing to create seamless transitions.

Exercise 3: Mixing with EQ

Objective: Learn how to use EQ (equalization) to blend tracks and create smooth mixes.

1. Select two tracks with matching BPMs.

2. Load one track onto each deck.

3. Start playing the first track and set the EQ to the default (12 o'clock position).

4. Start the second track on the other deck but keep the volume fader down.

5. As the second track begins playing, gradually increase the volume fader while using the EQ to

adjust the bass, midrange, and treble to complement the first track.

6. Pay attention to the EQ adjustments and volume levels to achieve a balanced mix.

7. Experiment with different EQ settings to create variations in your mixes.

Exercise 4: Adding Effects

Objective: Practice using effects to enhance your mixes.

1. Select two tracks and load them onto separate decks.

2. Choose an effect (e.g., reverb or delay) and load it onto one of the decks.

3. Start playing the first track without any effects.

4. Start the second track on the other deck.

5. When you want to add the effect, engage it on the deck where it's loaded.

6. Use the effect parameters (e.g., wet/dry mix) to control the intensity of the effect.

7. Experiment with different effects and their timing to create dynamic mixes.

Exercise 5: Advanced Mixing Techniques

Objective: Explore advanced mixing techniques like harmonic mixing and creative transitions.

1. Select two tracks with matching BPMs and compatible keys for harmonic mixing.
2. Load one track onto each deck.
3. Use harmonic mixing software or your ear to identify compatible keys.
4. Practice transitioning between the tracks using harmonic mixing techniques, such as mixing in key or key changes.
5. Experiment with creative transitions, such as backspins, echo drops, or filter sweeps, to add excitement to your mixes.
6. Record your practice sessions to review and refine your techniques.

Exercise 6: Crowd Interaction and Performance

Objective: Develop your crowd interaction and performance skills.

1. Set up a mock DJ performance with friends or in front of a mirror.

2. Select a setlist of tracks that build energy and mood.

3. Practice reading the imaginary crowd's reactions and adjusting your track selection and mixing style accordingly.

4. Incorporate performance techniques like looping, cue juggling, and scratching into your sets.

5. Engage with your imaginary audience, make eye contact, and use body language to convey energy and enthusiasm.

6. Record your practice performances and analyze them for improvement.

Routine: Daily Practice Session

Objective: Establish a daily practice routine to maintain and improve your DJing skills.

1. Allocate at least 30 minutes to 1 hour each day for practice.

2. Start with warm-up exercises like beatmatching and phrasing.

3. Work on a specific skill or technique during each practice session (e.g., beat juggling, harmonic mixing, or scratching).

4. Mix and match different tracks from your collection to keep things fresh and challenging.

5. Experiment with new music and genres to expand your repertoire.

6. Record your practice sessions and review them to track your progress.

7. Seek feedback from experienced DJs or mentors to gain insights and tips for improvement.

Remember that consistency is key to mastering the art of DJing. Regular practice and focused exercises will help you develop your skills, creativity, and confidence as a DJ.

About The Author

I didn't have a book like this when I started playing records in 1995. I had just come home from the Army and called up all my old skater buddies and said you guys still skating? My buddy

Jon said, "nope we're DJ's now". So, I went over to his house and watched what he was doing and was immediately hook. I gathered up all the money I had, took a drive down to Portland from Seattle (Oregon has no sales tax), and bought myself two Technic 1200's and a numark 2-channel mixer. I got as many records as I could with the money I had left and drove home. I grew up playing the drums so matching beats came easy, but there was no guidance on how to market myself. I recorded myself and handed out mixed tapes. I got some cool gigs and continued to grow in my craft. I left for college and played for another 10yrs. I continued to study the industry and have always loved House music and the art of DJing. I hope this manual can give some basic steps to help new DJ's on their road to

Made in the USA
Middletown, DE
18 October 2023

40992975R00133